GRACE UPON GRACE

A Memoir of my Treasures in Heaven

SHARLENE SCOTT

WESTBOW
PRESS®
A DIVISION OF THOMAS NELSON
& ZONDERVAN

WestBow Press books may be ordered through booksellers or by contacting:

WestBow Press
A Division of Thomas Nelson & Zondervan
1663 Liberty Drive
Bloomington, IN 47403
www.westbowpress.com
844-714-3454

ISBN: 978-1-6642-5655-2 (sc)
ISBN: 978-1-6642-5656-9 (hc)
ISBN: 978-1-6642-5657-6 (e)

Library of Congress Control Number: 2022901837

Print information available on the last page.

WestBow Press rev. date: 3/3/2022

Contents

1

Treasures

I learned early in life certain things about church.

You do not chew gum at church. I really think Mama told me it was against the law. I sat with a girl once who chewed gum, and I was afraid the police might come in, and she might end up in jail.

You gave money at church. A pastor from my childhood told me I started screaming in church once because the ushers didn't get my nickel when they passed the plate. He sent one of the ushers back to get my little offering. I don't remember that, but I do remember that after the offering we had prayer; and then we would leave the offering plates on a table. I thought that, while we were gone, angels came and got the money. We were giving it to God. How else was He supposed to get it?

When I was a child, we called the building the church house. I don't know how we got away from that, as it's really a better name than just church. I have learned that church (at its best) is a group of people doing life together—growing in their faith, being accountable to one another, and "rejoicing with them that do rejoice, and weeping with them that weep" (Romans 12:15). I cannot overemphasize the real value a church family has been in my life.

My parents met before World War II began, and although Daddy was still in high school, he volunteered for the army. He was captured in the Battle of the Bulge and was a prisoner in Germany for about four months. After the war, they were married in 1945 and had my brother, Rodney, in 1949. Sometime after Rodney was born, Mama and Daddy started listening to a preacher on the radio; both became Christians and began attending church.

Today, when I think of their faith, I remember the importance they placed on it. I remember that Daddy became a student of the Bible and continued to study his whole life. Mama loved music, and through the years, she told me about church songs she loved. If there were people they didn't like or they were in arguments with, they didn't tell us. Even as I write, reading the phrase "they were in arguments with" seems silly because I can't imagine such a thing with them. They both lived into their eighties and were able to celebrate their sixtieth wedding anniversary.

When I was older, Mama told me a story about Daddy cursing in German out the car window when he saw a group of Germans by the side of the road, apparently doing roadwork after the war. (Mama remembered as if it were normal after the war that we had German soldiers over here working, I think, as prisoners. I didn't know such a thing existed.) At the time, even more confounding was that Daddy would ever do something like that. Mama just said that the Lord had changed him. We always knew him as mild mannered and very caring. He liked to say he didn't care much for music, but he sang around the house all the time. So we learned the lyrics to most of Hank Williams's songs and other old country songs he liked. But more importantly, we learned a lot about Jesus at church, and at home, we could see what God could do in someone's life.

I don't remember ever not knowing about Jesus or not having church as an important part of our lives, and I am grateful for that.

My parents were never really strict. Daddy liked to say that his hope for his children was not indoctrination but for us to be thinking Christians. I think being a Christian brought a total change in Daddy.

I was young when I asked him a lot of questions about what it meant to get saved. One Sunday, I felt that God was calling me to be saved. There was no dramatic altar call and no fear of judgment. During the final hymn, I went down the aisle and told the preacher I wanted to get saved, and he said, "Stand beside me." After they finished the song, he announced to the church that I was a candidate for baptism and church membership. I remember during the song thinking I was so happy I might cry.

Here is what I did not know: I didn't know much about what I was doing. I didn't know the reason people needed to be saved. I certainly didn't understand that my sins separated me from God and that Jesus made the sacrifice to pay for my sins to end that separation. What I did know was that I had said yes to Jesus, and I was surprised by the joy I felt.

I learned later that many people had different experiences from mine. Usually, there was an explanation of what it was all about. Often, there was a prayer. Looking back, I'm glad it was so simple. As a teenager, I started questioning a lot of things, but I knew what had happened to me that night was something real that I could not forget. I could not blame it on a powerful speaker, on fear, or on being caught up in emotion. I knew it was simply a little girl meeting Jesus. The reality of that moment has been a steadying and motivating part of my life.

I no longer think that angels come and get the offerings we leave at church. But I have learned that angels do come and get some of our greatest treasures of all—our loved ones.

2

Granny

The very first treasure I remember losing was Granny Grady. When I was born, I had two living grandmothers. Both my grandfathers had passed away. Granny Grady, my maternal grandmother, was living with us. I don't know when she came. I can't remember before she came. She was widowed when Mama was about twelve. It seems to me that she mostly stayed in her room and always wore black dresses (that "memory" may have come from pictures we have). The main thing I remember about her is that she liked music. Mama told me that Granny loved to sing and had a beautiful voice. She said a man who grew up near them said he, as a child, liked to sit outside in the afternoon under their kitchen window and listen to Granny sing while she prepared dinner. Granny and I liked to watch the Lennon Sisters on *The Lawrence Welk Show* together. When I was a child, Janet Lennon was very young; she was much shorter than her sisters. Granny would call me to sit in her lap because we were going to hear "our girl" sing. My given first name was Janet, but I was never called that. I think that was part of what I liked about Janet Lennon. It was a little thing, but it's what I remember doing with Granny most.

One significant memory I have of her is about music. Our whole family is musically inclined. I majored in music in college. I have come to love all kinds of music as an adult. But the thing I love most in music, no matter what the style, is the joy of harmonizing—like the Lennon Sisters did.

Granny died when I was in the second grade. Just before she died, Mama and Daddy had brought home some papers from the hospital. One of them was about telling your children about the death of family members. I read it and felt I was in on some big adult secret. When they told me Granny had passed, I thought, *They think I don't get it, but I do.* I felt very grown up. I didn't cry. I think I may have smiled a little because I was thinking about how mature I was.

Her funeral was on Christmas Day—Christmas Day! I've been told the reasoning behind this was that so many out-of-town relatives would be here. Anyway, my cousin was going to stay at our house with my sister Melanie, who was only two, and I was supposed to go to the funeral. I did cry then. I wanted to stay home and play with my new toys. Looking back, I probably pitched a very rude fit. I did get to stay home. But later I would remember this and feel guilty. I was an adult before I forgave myself.

I never talked to anyone about the way I reacted to Granny's death and especially about the fact that I cried to keep from going to the funeral. I was too ashamed. Later, I wondered that I had not been more affected by her death. Now, of course, I realize I was affected for years by it, but I was never willing to deal with it because I felt so guilty. I know there are lots of children affected, like me, in unusual (and often much more serious) ways by the tragedies in their lives. Some of them are scarred for life, but they never tell anyone. Today, we tend to ask our children more about their feelings. But if anyone had asked me then, I don't know that I would have told them anything, especially not my parents. I just carried the guilt for a long time.

I suppose every death affects us in more ways than we know. Every life, short or long, has an impact on us.

3

Paul and Me

In my early twenties, I learned about Paul. His parents attended our church, and Paul was in the hospital and had nearly died from complications from type 1 diabetes. But he became a Christian in the hospital, and the ladies in our women's auxiliary bought him a Living Bible.

When he got out of the hospital, Paul started coming to church. He kind of looked like a hippie, although it was 1979. I had a weird sort of respect for his long hair look. It wasn't in style, but I thought it displayed an "I-don't-want-to-sell-out" attitude, sort of a holdover from the hippie days. Even to me, that makes little sense now. But at the time, I thought it did. (It wasn't his motive, though. He told me later girls always told him he had pretty hair, and he did.)

One Sunday night at church, Paul went to the altar and prayed. He spoke with the preacher. This particular preacher liked to pray for people out loud and often repeated whatever they had told him. I always thought, if I ever had something big to confess, I'd be afraid to tell him.

But what the preacher said that night was, "This young man says he's been following God part of the way, but he wants to follow Him all the way." I was very moved by this. So many people are part-time Christians. It was refreshing to see someone who really wanted to be committed to God. So, I decided I had a mission to encourage him in his faith. Really, that's all I was thinking at that point.

A few months later, he got a haircut. It was his gift to his mother for Christmas. I was very moved by this, for a few reasons. Mainly, he looked very good. Now my resolve to encourage him really grew, except now my reason was a little different.

Over time, I did come to know Paul better—every chance I got. For a while, our "relationship" consisted of one thing. After church on Sunday mornings, while people were standing around talking outside, Paul and I would have brief conversations. Over time, I saw him at other events, and we became good friends. I think everyone knew I was interested in more than friendship, but for a long time, nothing changed. My roommate and I started a Bible study at our apartment, and one of the people we invited was Paul. He always came, and he and I got to talk a lot.

Paul and I were both in the church Christmas play that year, and we both had to sing. Paul was not really a singer and asked me to help him with his song. So, we had that time together. December brought my twenty-sixth birthday. A lady at church heard someone wish me a happy birthday, and she asked how old I was. When I told her, she said, "Don't worry. I was older than that before I got married." I don't remember my response, but I remember that it made me angry that she assumed I would be worried about turning twenty-six without a husband. I was bothered by women who judged each other's value, and their own, on whether or not they got married by a certain age— or at all. I became a little militant about that, as God has a purpose for each of us, whether or not that includes marriage.

Paul gave me a birthday card that said something about what a great Christian friend I was. I didn't like that "friend" phrase, although becoming friends was probably the best way to start a relationship. But the card said, for my gift, he would take me to see the movie *Stir Crazy*. I had "casually" mentioned I wanted to see it. So, our first date was December 22. The next night, we went to a Christmas Communion at my roommate's church. Then we became inseparable.

One night in January, he told me one of our friends had told him I really didn't care if I ever got married or not. I knew it was because of my rantings about marriage. But I had always hoped I would get married, and even more so after Paul came along. I explained what I meant.

A week later, he gave me an envelope with a small jigsaw puzzle in it. I put the pieces together and it said, "Will you marry me?" It was almost a month after our first date.

When we went to tell our parents, we went out to dinner and rode around, chewing on Rolaids, trying to get up our nerve to tell them. I don't know that I expected them to be upset, but it was so soon after we had started dating. Or course, they were all very supportive. We got married in June.

4

Miracles

When I met Paul, he had only been drug-free since he'd become a Christian the previous year. Drugs, especially heroin, had been a big part of his life for several years. He was a juvenile diabetic, so it was even more dangerous for him to be involved in drugs. Still, I think diabetes may have saved him. Whenever he was really getting into trouble with drugs, he was paying no attention to his diabetic care, and he would end up having to go to the hospital.

The last time he went into the hospital (during that period) was the time he got the Living Bible from our church. He really had ended up there because of drugs, which complicated his diabetes. There was a preacher who was in the room beside him. The preacher asked Paul if he could pray about anything for him. Paul's mother would come to visit and cry, which made him mad, and it would turn into an argument. Then Paul would feel terrible after she left. Paul asked the preacher to pray that he and his mother would not fight when she visited. The prayer was answered. But by that time, Paul had a new idea.

He had been in the hospital enough that he had learned all the tricks. His plan was to request pain medicine at every opportunity but not take it. He kept the pills hidden, with a plan to take them all on Saturday for a great high. He kept the plan, but after taking the pills, nothing happened. He couldn't understand it but somehow felt sure God was reaching out to him. So, finally, he prayed. He told God he needed to see Him, and he needed to see a miracle.

Paul went to sleep that night and suddenly woke up because he thought someone had come into his room. He was sure whoever had entered had turned on the light and then quickly turned it off. He got up and went to the door to see who it was, but no one was around. He called his nurse, who assured him no one had been in his room. Somehow, he knew it was God. He knew it was God who had taken away the effects of the drugs. He knew that, if he was going to continue to live, he would have to depend on God. This was the beginning of his new life.

As he prepared to leave the hospital, he remembered he had prayed for a miracle. He told God, *I still haven't seen a miracle.*

Then he looked in the mirror and realized the miracle was him.

Later, I asked Paul what had made him get involved in drugs. He said it was peer pressure. Coming from a military family, he'd changed schools many times and often had to make new friends in the middle of the school year. He made friends with a pretty wild group when he came to Goldsboro. He started doing what his friends were doing, and that involved smoking pot. Then his popularity grew when his friends found out that he (a diabetic) had access to lots of clean needles. This led him to a new group of friends and a new habit.

5

Married Life

After Paul's dad retired from the military, they settled in Goldsboro, and Paul went to Goldsboro High School where I attended. It was a big school, and we never met. Later, we found out we both knew some of the same people, but we hung out in very different circles.

But when we met in our mid-twenties at church, we shared the same priorities, although we had come to that point from really different backgrounds.

So, Paul and I were married quickly, and were crazy in love. Paul had been married before. His ex-wife had moved with their son, Shawn, to Washington State, where her husband was from. They came for a visit just before we got married, so I got to meet Shawn.

Paul and I were determined to have a Christian marriage, but we hardly knew each other and had surprisingly different outlooks on almost everything.

Paul had little church experience. He told me he'd been invited to a Sunday school class party one evening before we got together. Some of the men were talking, and one confessed that his son had repeated a bad word, and he knew he had heard it from him. When Paul told me that story, I said, "Oh, he never should have said that in front of a brand-new Christian like you!" But Paul said, "No! I was glad he did! I had put Christians on a pedestal, and I realized they were real ordinary people like me."

Paul was amazed by the grace of God. He saw miracles in commonplace things. In some ways, I thought of him as larger than life. Everything that happened was the most amazing thing to him. He was fascinated by so many things as a young Christian. He couldn't understand why we all weren't constantly as excited as he was. He was always much more emotional than I was. I sometimes marveled at his different insight into the Christian life. When we were first dating, he told me about a "new" discovery he had made about God's love. He said when he told his parents about it, they told him he needed to calm down a little.

Paul's favorite scripture was Psalm 150. He memorized it from the Living Bible. One day, our car broke down, and we had to wait to have someone come about thirty miles to tow the car to a shop. I was sitting in the car thinking about how much this was going to cost. Paul was reciting Psalm 150 from the Living Bible:

> Hallelujah!
> Yes, Praise the Lord!
> Praise Him in His temple, and in the heavens he made with mighty power.
> Praise Him for His mighty works.
> Praise His unequaled greatness.
> Praise Him with the trumpet, and with lute and harp.
> Praise Him with the tambourines and processional.
> Praise Him with stringed instruments and horns.
> Praise Him with the cymbals, yes, loud clanging cymbals.

Let everything alive give praise to the Lord!
You praise Him!
Hallelujah!

His favorite song was "The Old Rugged Cross." When he was young, he heard this song at his grandmother's funeral, so for him it had always been a sad song. But then he became a Christian and listened to the words, and he realized this was not bad news but, rather, the best news of all! The cross had become, for him, something wonderful.

One Sunday night at church, someone sang it. Paul's sister was there, and when the song started, she got up and was going out, in tears over this sad song. Paul followed her and made her listen to it. He wanted her to understand the meaning he'd found in it.

He was eager to help. Years later, a friend told me about a Christmas when their son was small and wanted a particular toy that was in great demand. She'd been unable to find it, but Paul had seen it somewhere and picked it up for her. Probably, he'd looked everywhere for it. He loved to help whenever he could and would work harder to help someone else than he would to help himself. I learned early that, if you told Paul you needed a particular item from the store, he would go to every store in town until he found exactly what you wanted. He just loved helping people.

This was never truer than at Christmastime. If we had been a little richer, I can't imagine how much he would have spent on gifts. He could hardly sleep on Christmas Eve, because he couldn't wait to give away the gifts he'd selected. He really understood the joy of giving.

Still, there was another side to that coin. Paul took negative things to heart as well. If there was a problem, it was a terrible problem. If there was a disagreement, he wanted to talk it out until we agreed. He never felt that agreeing to disagree was OK. He could get angry very quickly, and just as quickly, he would be over it. I was not so quick to anger and, once I was angry, not so quick to forget. We joked that, between us, we were like God. I was slow to anger, and Paul was quick to forgive.

We struggled sometimes to understand each other, but I think our commitment to have a Christian marriage was the glue that made us keep working at it.

6

Learning Diabetes

I knew so little about diabetes before marrying Paul. But I learned gradually.

Low blood sugars were most frightening to me, and other people as well. Thomas, a friend from church, asked Paul to go with him to visit a family who had a son with a drug problem. They weren't sure if they would see the son or not on the visit, but they could at least talk with the parents, and Paul could share his story. Apparently, Paul's blood sugar had dropped, and he never spoke while they were talking to the parents. Thomas tried to prompt him with questions, and he didn't answer.

Fortunately, the lady asked if Paul was diabetic. When Thomas said yes, she got him something to eat, and he, very gradually, came around. On their way home, Paul said to Thomas, "I know I should know this, but what is your name?"

We were thankful this lady had recognized the problem. We smiled at the irony of someone coming to help a drug addict but unable to remember anything or hold a conversation.

Paul was often able to tell when his blood sugar was getting low, but that got worse over time. During the early days of our marriage, he didn't have a glucometer to check blood sugars. We had scares, but nothing serious ever happened because of these occasional dips in blood sugar levels.

7

A New Adventure

After two years of marriage (and once we had our insurance right), Paul and I decided to start our family. During that time, an acquaintance of ours had three healthy children and then had a miscarriage (twins). We went to visit her, and she talked on and on about how angry she was at God for this happening to her. It wasn't right. It wasn't fair. How could God be so cruel? They were just innocent babies.

I had mixed feelings listening to all this. I wanted to stop what she was saying. It was like she was saying terrible things about my friend, and I wanted to come to His defense. But I had heard that anger was part of grieving, and so I thought we should just let her get it out, which is what I did.

Soon, I learned I was pregnant. In those days, we didn't have home pregnancy tests, or maybe I was too cheap to buy one. I went to the health department, took a test, and then had to wait for them to call me in a couple of weeks at a certain time. Paul was at work when the time came, but almost as soon as I found out, I saw his truck flying into our front yard. I ran outside, and said, "Hey, Daddy." We both cried for the longest time. We were so excited. We told everyone right away.

Near the end of my second month, I started spotting. I went to the doctor, and he did an ultrasound and said I was having a miscarriage. On the scan, he showed me the sack. He said it had grown with the baby, and it was the right size for how far along I was. But there was no baby inside. He told me something must have happened to the baby earlier. He said, "Give it a few days, and you will pass everything." He told me there was no reason not to go to work. So, I did, thinking staying home and stressing over it would be harder than working, and he said it wouldn't make any difference. Of course, I was sad when I was working, so either way, it was bad. One of my coworkers said her doctor would have tried to save that baby. So, I had some guilt to add to my sadness. On Saturday afternoon, I started cramping and bleeding a lot. We went to the hospital, and I had a D&C. The doctor told me afterwards that there was no fetal tissue in what they'd removed.

Word got around at church, and several women stopped by to visit me, some telling me they had also suffered a miscarriage. In the next weeks, I heard the same from more women. I had no idea how common it was. What was most helpful in hearing their stories was that most of them went on to have more healthy pregnancies. Our stories matter, and we need to share them.

I wrote in my journal, "I don't feel angry about what has happened. All I feel is sad." I did not write that I must have been a more mature Christian than my friend who had been so angry with God, and that is why she'd experienced anger that I did not. But that was what I was thinking. I'm not proud of that thought now, but it was how I felt at that point.

8

Matthew

After the miscarriage, we were told to wait three months to try again. We waited until Christmas Eve. Paul and I stayed up late and opened all our presents. We had a wonderful Christmas, and I believe we made a baby that night. Because of the miscarriage, we didn't tell anyone for a while this time.

The big warning to pregnant women at that time was not to get in contact with cat feces, because it could cause some sort of poison to the baby's system. My sister asked me to go with her to take her cat to the vet. The cat was sick and actually had diarrhea all over my jeans. When we left the vet's office, I started crying. So, then I had to tell her what that was about.

I went home and took a long shower and cried and cried. I asked the Lord to give me some assurance that this baby would be born healthy, but I never got any such assurance. I went to the doctor the next day and told him what had happened. He was not at all concerned; he said a baby being harmed by cat feces was very rare, and people were making too much of it.

My pregnancy was not affected by the cat at all. But there was something else in store for us.

Another incident frightened me, although God's hand was clearly in it. We were renting our house. For Paul's birthday, his mother gave him a renter's insurance policy. I thought at the time, *What kind of birthday present is this?*

However, I thought very differently two days later. On Monday night, I woke up to the smell of smoke. I turned on the lamp by the bed and couldn't see anything.

I told Paul, "Something's on fire."

He said, "Turn on the light."

"It's on!"

We ran through the house. Paul found the fire in the kitchen. We had a galley kitchen and it was too small for a table, but Paul had attached half a table top to the wall. It was cooler-looking than this sounds. Anyway, a candle on the table had been left burning and had caught the table and the wall on fire. Paul yanked the table from the wall and threw it into the backyard. Then he put the fire out and told me to go out on the porch. Since I was pregnant, he didn't want me smelling the smoke. We called the fire department, mainly to make sure there was no fire in the attic or anything. Paul struck me as very strong during the incident. But he said, when he called the fire department, they'd told him to calm down so they could understand him.

After they left, Paul came out to the porch and sat with me, and we prayed. I had already figured out I had left the candle burning on the table. I told Paul, and he was really sweet about it—although, for a long time, he didn't want us to burn candles in our house. But that was OK with me. I felt the same way.

After the fire, I took a shower, again praying about my baby. I got out and dried myself off with the towel and looked in the mirror. My face was still covered in smoke (from the towel). Paul called his parents and told them what had happened. We went over to their house (for second showers), and his dad met us at the door. Looking at us, he said, "I see nothing of value was lost." I reminded myself of that so many times in the coming months.

I went to the doctor the next day and told him about the fire and all the smoke in the house. He said he would be more worried if I had told him I smoked a cigarette that night. So I felt better about that. We called our landlord, who lived out of state. They decided they were going to sell the house. They told us to get our things out, so they could get ready to sell. We were given permission to store some things at an old building at our church and other things at our parents' homes. We mostly stayed at Paul's parents' house. We had also stayed at my parents' house, and some church friends invited us over for a weekend at their house.

Sometimes, we would joke about that period of time when we were homeless. But, although we were temporarily without a house, we always had places to stay. It did make me think of families who, for whatever reason, lost their homes and did not have relatives or friends nearby who were willing and able to let them stay with them. In those days, we were hearing about families who were homeless. I heard people say that these people probably had problems because of their lifestyles. We have no idea about most of them. And if it is their fault, so what? If you're homeless, you're homeless. What if Paul and I had moved far away before our small house fire? We could have been in the same boat. I hope I keep the compassion I learned from that.

During those days, my extra time was spent washing all the dishes, towels, and curtains from our house. We were able to have everything we couldn't wash ourselves professionally cleaned—thanks to that little insurance policy. It also helped us with our down payment on our house, so it turned about to be a great birthday present for Paul. We found a realtor and looked at lots of houses. We applied for a loan from a company our realtor had recommended. Later, I told a woman from church who had experience with such things that we'd found a house. Her advice was not to go with a particular loan company, as they were slow and getting approved always took a long time with them. By then, we had signed the papers, and it was too late. But she was right. After a few months, the homeowner said if we didn't get the loan approved by the end of June, she would put it back on the market. At that point, our loan was approved in a few days.

My sister became engaged during that time, so there were fun times planning the wedding, attending showers, looking for bridesmaids' dresses, and wondering how fat the pregnant matron of honor would be by the time of the wedding (as it turned out, too fat for the dress we ordered, so Mama made me a dress and it looked perfect. She made Melanie's beautiful wedding dress too. One would think that might motivate me to learn to be a good seamstress like my Mom, but no). Looking at houses and planning weddings are fun and joyful times. There are always things to rejoice about—if we look for them.

One day, I told Paul, "Here we are having a baby, with no house to set up a nursery in."

He said, "I was thinking, we're going to have a new house! We're going to have a new baby! Shawn is coming from Washington for a visit in June! We have so much to look forward to!"

That helped me get a new perspective.

My pregnancy progressed normally, for all I knew. I had some morning sickness, but not too much. In June, I went for a checkup. I told the doctor we were planning to go to the mountains that week. He assured me it would be fine. I felt good and was excited. Shawn had come, and we were taking him camping. We had a nice trip, although I had some swelling in my feet. I'd been told you can expect that to happen when you're pregnant in the summer. We came home on Saturday, and when we went to church on Sunday, a nurse there told me maybe I should check with my doctor the next day. The swelling was worse that day, and she thought I might have preeclampsia (I had never heard of such a thing).

On Monday morning, we closed on our house at the lawyer's

office. On Monday afternoon, I went to the doctor. I still felt fine, but now the swelling was even worse. When the nurse saw me, she took my blood pressure, which was very high. She asked if I had a headache, but I really felt fine.

They sent me straight to the hospital. The doctor said, "I'll call your husband. Don't go home to get anything. Go straight to the ER."

I protested that I was driving my parents' car.

But he said, "They can get their car later."

I cried all the way to the hospital. The ER staff didn't know what to do with me, so they sent me to admitting. Admitting didn't know what to do either, so they sent me up to labor and delivery. They were expecting me and seemed somewhat casual about everything. They put me in a room and said, "Let's get that blood pressure down." I felt encouraged by their attitude, and when Paul came, I told him I may have to be here a day or two to get my blood pressure down, but I felt fine. He said, "This is very serious."

I guess I wanted him not to worry, so I said, "I know. But we'll be fine." And I really thought that was true—until they told me about my blood pressure. The only symptom I had noticed was the swelling of my feet, and I knew that could happen a lot in the summer.

They put me on an IV to help lower the blood pressure. My doctor said it was severe preeclampsia, and the only cure was delivery. I was twenty-four weeks pregnant. Of course, we knew it was way too soon to deliver. I said, "I'll stay in the hospital until October" (our due date) "if I need to. I'll just lay right here."

Then he explained that, if I was sick, the baby would be sick as well. We were both at risk. He also said at this stage, if they had to deliver, the baby would have about a 50 percent chance of surviving birth.

They took me down to have an ultrasound. I kept dozing off. When we were looking at the baby, I asked about fingers and toes, and the doctor said they were not concerned about that. I heard the guy who took me back up to my room telling someone I kept falling asleep. I didn't know if they thought that was a bad sign or what, but mostly I still kept dozing in and out. (Drugs? Denial? I don't know).

The following morning, they sent me to Chapel Hill, which had an excellent neonatal intensive care unit. I don't remember much about the ambulance ride or much else that day. The doctors at Chapel Hill continued to try to lower my blood pressure all day, but nothing changed. My swelling continued to increase. Daddy said later that he had walked by my room at the hospital because he didn't recognize the patient—which was me! That evening, they started trying to induce labor. I felt some mild contractions, but they weren't really painful. It kind of felt like bad cramps. One time, the nurse asked if I knew I was having contractions. I remember thinking, *If this is all that labor is, women are wimps.* I know that's not true.

Late that night, I was being prepared for a C-section. The baby's heart rate had slowed down, and something had to be done. I had the choice of being put to sleep or numbed. And before I could say, "Put me to sleep!" the nurse said, "Of course, putting you to sleep is more dangerous for the baby." So, of course, it was a no-brainer. I stayed awake.

Matthew was born June 26 at 12:55 a.m. I was in the OR with an anesthesiologist at one shoulder repeatedly asking me if I could feel this or that. Paul was on the other side, mostly telling me he loved me. Of course, I couldn't see anything that was going on, which was probably a good thing. Paul had been a little grossed out looking at natural childbirth pictures, and I had told him he didn't have to go in with me, but he insisted. He was very wonderful. I heard Matthew's first cry. Paul was surprised I could hear it. I guess it was a little gift from God. I wrote in my journal that God must have done that for me, because He knew it would be a long time before I heard Matthew's voice again.

The next few days were something of a blur to me. Family members came. Our wedding anniversary was June 28, so Rodney and Gale took Paul out for lunch to celebrate. When they came back, Paul told me about the restaurant and wished I could have been there.

I said, "Don't feel bad. I had a bowl of chicken broth."

Mostly I was still very drowsy. Matthew was so early we hadn't settled on a name for the baby yet, and I was pretty much out of it when they asked. I wanted Matthew Paul, and Paul had wanted Joshua Paul. So, when they asked for a name, he gave them Matthew Joshua, (Later, someone commented how we had chosen an Old Testament name and a New Testament name, but really it just happened that way). Matthew weighed one pound and ten ounces. I learned new words like Apgar scores. The nurses told me his score at one minute was 1, but at five minutes it was 6, which apparently was still not good. I didn't know the difference, which was probably a good thing. I learned much later that most healthy babies begin with a score of at least 7, and at 5 minutes, it should be 10.

Matthew was immediately put on a respirator (or vent) and went to the NICU (neonatal intensive care unit). I didn't get to see him for a couple of days because I was so sick. Matthew's primary nurse, Anne, was just great. She came to my room to tell me about Matthew. She described for me what to expect when I saw him, because the NICU could be scary. I asked what color his eyes were, and she casually said, "Oh, they're not open yet." I just thought that must be a common thing among preemies. Later, I learned that the nurses in NICU felt that, when a baby's eyes weren't open at birth, this baby was probably too young to live. I'm glad they didn't tell me that at the time. His blue eyes didn't open until July 9.

The hospital was eighty miles from home. On Wednesday night, Paul had to go home. I hated so much to see him go. But he came back the next day, and I finally was able to get out of ICU and go to a room. When Paul and the nurses wheeled me out, they let me stop at the NICU and see Matthew for the first time. I had been told a lot about what to expect when I got there. But it was still a great shock for me. It was really bright and noisy in there. There were no cribs.

The babies were in clear plastic trays, naked under these bright lights, called bili lights, to keep up their body temperatures. When we went in, we had to wash our hands and put on hospital gowns.

As he wheeled me in, Paul pointed to one of the trays and said, "There he is."

I looked over there. "I don't see him." I saw something in there, but it was way too small to be a baby, I thought. But it was him. I was so shocked when I saw him, I cried a little.

I wrote in my journal, "The nurses were encouraging. They [and Paul] treated him like a real normal baby. They told me to touch him, and they all talked to him like any other baby. I was almost afraid to hope for him. But Paul was already crazy over him, and he made it easier for me."

Paul stayed all weekend. He wheeled me down to see the baby frequently. Sometimes, he'd just take me around the hospital. During the day, he stayed in my room most of the time. After I started to adjust to the shock of what had happened, I felt so grateful that Matthew had made it so far. On Sunday, Paul took me to the worship service in the hospital chapel. We sang the song "For the Beauty of the Earth." One line said, "For the love which from our birth over and around us lies … Lord of all to thee we raise this our hymn of grateful praise." I was so overwhelmed with the knowledge that God saw all that was going on and that He loved Matthew. That's the only thing I remember about the service, except for crying a lot.

When Paul went back home to go to work on Monday, my sister, Melanie, came and stayed with me. She and Johnny had only been married a month, and I felt bad taking her away from her new husband, but I was very happy to have her around.

I had assumed breastfeeding was out, since I had not gone full term, and Matthew was on a vent. But I did start producing milk, and the nurses suggested I use a breast pump and save the milk for him, even after I went home. I'd had access to an electric pump at the hospital, and it was pretty easy to use. I went home with a hand pump, which was a *lot* of work for very little milk. But I had been assured by the nurses that my milk, even if it was only a small amount, was the best thing I could give Matthew, and I was so happy to be able to do something for him.

I went home on July 4. I felt very loved. When we got home to our new house, members of our family and our church family were moving our stuff in. I just sat and told people where I wanted things to go. That was kind of fun, but it was weird. I felt like everyone I knew was going through all my things. But mostly, I felt grateful for their kindness. It was a holiday, but instead of going to the beach, they were all volunteering their time for us.

I received a lot of cards, mostly the "thinking of you" cards and even sympathy cards. My cousin Joyce sent a beautiful card congratulating me on my new baby boy. It was perfect and gave me joy.

I had problems with my incision and went home with it not completely sewn up. The nurses taught me to clean and pack it once a day. It was difficult for me because of the location, and I needed a mirror to do it. Paul held the mirror for me the third day, and watched, and said, "Oh, I can do that for you." I was surprised and felt very loved.

On Sunday, we went to church, and after the worship service, my pastor called me into his office. I was serving, at that time, as organist and choir director and youth choir director, and I taught a Sunday school class. Mr. Ard told me that people would let you work until you dropped, but he wasn't going to let that happen to me. I had a long, tough road ahead of me, and I needed to focus on that and not worry about my responsibilities at church. I was ready to tell him I could handle everything. But before I could say it, he told me he had already given other people all my jobs. I didn't understand then what a gift he was giving me, and I wouldn't have done it had he given me a choice.

I felt useless. I had a new baby and a new house, and I couldn't take care of either. I was recovering still and couldn't go to work yet.

I had no responsibilities at church anymore. But then, I thought of all those precious babies in NICU and how valued they were, and they couldn't *do* anything. They couldn't even breathe without help. Our value is because we are loved. And we're all loved by God.

A standard answer in a neonatal intensive care unit was that the caregivers try to enable babies to be strong enough to come home on their due date. Matthew was born June 26, but his due date was not until October. I hated to imagine him being in the hospital for that long.

Shawn had to fly back to Washington soon, but I was glad he got to see Matthew. It must have been a strange adventure for him during those days, but he adapted well.

9

The Ride Begins

Matthew weighed one pound ten ounces at birth but lost an ounce right away. We were told that was not unusual. We learned quickly about the obstacles he faced. The big one was the fact that his lungs were so undeveloped. He started out on a ventilator, and the goal was to help him gain weight and strength and gradually get off the vent and breathe on his own. The problem was a vent kept him from learning to use a bottle, and his nourishment had to come from an IV. Another problem with the vent was the damage it could do to the lungs. Babies who suffer from this have bronchopulmonary dysplasia (BPD). We learned that babies like him were susceptible to infections because they were so weak and didn't have fully developed immune systems to fight anything. His weight, his oxygen levels, and the amount of pressure he needed from the ventilator to be able to breathe became important things to watch. Even with all that, we felt that God had a plan, and we were trusting Him for a miracle for our baby.

Someone told us about a preemie baby clothing store at the mall.

So we went. But the clothes were much too big for Matthew. I had to leave the store. I was stunned and weeping. I think it really hit me that day how tiny our baby was and how serious our situation was. But Mama made him some cute clothes that would fit. I was grateful, and it was probably good for Mama as well.

When he was two weeks old, Matthew looked a little puffy. Almost as soon as we got to the nursery, the nurses told us the doctor needed to see us. He told us Matthew had an infection and was still quite weak; they weren't sure he would be able to fight it. He doubted that Matthew would be able to pull through. But we kept praying and hoping anyway.

That meeting was on Wednesday, and on Saturday, we had to meet with two doctors and a nurse. This time, they said his lung disease was bad. No oxygen was going into his blood, and they didn't know what else they could do for him. They pretty much gave him a couple of days.

That night, we came back to Goldsboro and went to see our parents and told them the news. I thought I could be strong and tell them, but I fell apart. When we got back home, our pastor came to see us. He told us the story of King David and his first son he had with Bathsheba (II Samuel 12:15–23). The baby was dying, and David, who was very upset, pleaded with God to save him. But the baby did die, and the people who had been around David were worried about telling him, as he was already so distraught.

But David didn't fall apart. He didn't lose his faith in God. Instead, after learning the news, he got up and went and worshiped the Lord. He said, "I shall go to him, but he shall not return to me."

I think Mr. Ard was trying to emphasize that even if our baby passed away, we would see him in heaven one day. There was a little comfort in that, but I wasn't ready to give up on Matthew.

I could not sleep that night and prayed for the longest time. At first, I felt that, if I prayed for his healing, and then he died, where would my faith be? I guess I was thinking that God might say no to my prayer, and if He did, I might lose faith in prayer altogether. What would be the point? But then, I thought about King David praying until he learned that the answer was no, and then he went and worshiped God. I thought, *I will do that.* So, I spent much of the night in prayer, pleading for my son. I eventually fell asleep.

When I woke the next morning, I had great peace. I had no idea what was going to happen. I just felt at peace.

We got to the nursery that morning, and the nurse said Matthew had had kind of a turnaround. She couldn't believe he was so much better. We were, of course, overjoyed. We felt God had done a miracle. And this would be the first of many.

10

The Black Hand

God loves to send the right people at the right time. Not long before Matthew was born, my college roommate's husband got a job in Goldsboro, where we lived. Rack, as we always called her, had two young children. Her oldest, Michael, was a preemie. Although not born as early as Matthew was, Michael had spent some time in a NICU before he could go home.

One day, during Matthew's first month in the hospital, I was with Rack and another mother, who said, "You know, Matthew will always be way too small for his age and will always be behind other kids developmentally. That's the way it is for preemies."

I had heard differently about that but didn't say anything. I thought, *What do I know?* And I also thought, *Why would she say that to me?*

Rack didn't say anything either but called me later that day. She told me that preemies are not expected to stay behind. They should grow normally. Even more reassuring to me was the fact that her son, Michael, was now older and in the normal size range for his age. He was developing in every way normally.

The next day, Rack and I were on the phone. She told me a story from when Michael was a baby. Preemies have lots of IVs and tubes and such all the time when they're in NICU. There had been an IV in Michael's foot. It was wrapped up, and when they went to change the IV, they found that his foot had turned black. Apparently, his foot wasn't getting oxygen because of the IV, and they feared he could lose his foot but thought probably he would only lose a toe or two. However, in a few hours, his circulation improved, and everything was fine.

That same day (no kidding), I called the hospital to check on Matthew. The nurses told me that his hand was black. It was the same story and the same prognosis I had heard earlier that day from my friend. The results were also the same. I was amazed at having heard this story at that time. I felt God had to have reminded Rack of that particular incident. I was not at all afraid, and everything came out fine.

I think Rack telling me that story was the hand of God. II Corinthians 1:3–4 says, "Blessed be God, even the Father of our Lord Jesus Christ, the Father of mercies, and the God of all comfort; Who comforteth us in all our tribulation, *that we may be able to comfort* them which are in any trouble, by the comfort wherewith we ourselves are comforted of God" (italics mine). God used what had happened to Rack to help me. Things like this reminded me that the God of grace was there with us. Things like this also made me feel Matthew would eventually be just fine and would soon be a normal, healthy child. I forgot that God's ways are not our ways.

11

One Step Forward, Two Steps Back

A couple of weeks passed, and Matthew seemed to be improving. One of the doctors called his condition "critically stable." His infection was gone. His hand was fine. But his need for maximum settings had continued. I asked the doctor if he felt like things were more hopeful than they had been two weeks before. He said, "Not really." He said they would have to try gradually, bit by bit, to lower Matthew's ventilator settings. He called it "sink or swim."

They were able to lower the settings a little each day, and things were going well for about a week. Then Matthew got sick, and everything went back up to the maximum settings.

On one visit, one of the NICU nurses showed me another baby who had been there for nine months. He would be there several more months before he would be able to go home. I thought, *How sad for this family.* Then she said, "This is the best you can expect for

Matthew." I had been imagining Matthew home by Christmas, but now that seemed like a ridiculous hope.

On August 5, Matthew's primary nurse, Anne, called to say they'd lowered his pressure from the vent to twenty-three, and his breaths per minute from thirty-eight to thirty. She said, "In one day, he made about a month's progress."

We were thrilled, and I began again to hope for Christmas.

12

Miracles along the Way

Our first house payment was due about a month after Matthew's birth. I was still out of work, and I got a little worried about the financial strain. During the first month, I got an unexpected check from the IRS. There had been a mistake on our tax return. One Sunday morning at church, a woman handed Paul an envelope with some money to help us. He told me after church, and I thought how wonderfully God supplies our needs. Then Paul told me he gave it for offering! I would not have done that, but now it was too late. I had not expected any money from my job, because I had not been working. But the next day, I got a check for whatever time I had worked before going in the hospital.

There would be many times when people in our family or people at church would give us money. Sometimes, we got checks in the mail from people we hardly knew. I would love to tell you we never worried about finances anymore because of it, but it's not true. Still, God was faithful to us. I wrote in my journal, "So the same God who did all that will take care of Matthew and our future."

13

In for the Long Haul

We had heard about tracheotomies and had seen a couple of babies who had them. But we were so sure Matthew was going to steadily improve that we didn't think about them too much. Then in September, the doctor announced that Matthew would be having surgery the next day to do a tracheotomy. He said Matthew could be on oxygen for a couple of years, and with a "trach," he would be able to eat. Otherwise, he may forget how to eat and have trouble ever learning how. Also, once he was off the respirator, he could wear a trach collar, and it would give him a lot more freedom.

I could see the doctors were not looking for the miracles we were hoping for. Still, we trusted their wisdom, and the surgery went fine.

One of the babies died that week. He was ten months old. He was the one who had been there so long—the one the nurse had shown as an example of the best Matthew could hope for. It was very discouraging. But I never let myself dwell too long on negative possibilities. I thought of that as living by faith, and I still think that's part of it. I know it can also be denial, and that's definitely a factor for me.

I went back to work. Since we couldn't be there every day, Matthew was given a lap mom, Ana. She was a volunteer who came whenever we weren't there and held Matthew and rocked him. When he was able to take a bottle, she would help feed him too.

It was hard to think that someone else was doing my job. But at the same time, it was wonderful to know that someone was there every day—just for the purpose of loving Matthew. And she was very sweet and really loved him.

I mentioned once to our doctors, "What if I quit my job and come up here to live near Matthew?"

Paul would have had to stay back home for his job, and honestly, I have no idea how I thought we would be able to finance such an endeavor. But the doctors said that many couples with a sick child divorced. Paul and I needed to stay in the same place. I knew it was the right thing to do, but I felt guilty when we had to leave Matthew so far away.

14

The Thrill of the Ride

By October, Matthew was up to three pounds and nine ounces (every ounce counts when you're that size). We felt he was progressing well. But his original due date came and went with no possibility of going home. His lungs were starting to show development. The doctors were not pleased that his weight gain was slow. He was older and more alert and moved around a lot and was learning to play a little, so they started sedating him so he would sleep at night and not burn so many calories.

The big news was that they were planning to start trying him on a trach collar, which meant for periods at a time, he would not be on the vent at all, just oxygen.

On October 16, Anne, called to tell us Matthew had been on the trach collar that day for an hour and had tolerated it fine. He'd spent the hour breathing on his own! I was so excited I was jumping up and down in the kitchen. Paul was just sitting at the table with his head down. I couldn't believe it! "Aren't you excited?" He could hardly answer me because he was crying.

Matthew had been in isolation because of an infection, but it had cleared up. Now he was in an actual crib! By the end of October, he was on the trach collar for up to four hours a day and weighed over four pounds. He had started reaching for things with his hands and smiled a lot. Paul played with him more than anyone else, and when Paul would hold him, Matthew's whole attitude seemed to change, as if he knew it was playtime. We had even been allowed to push him around the hospital in his stroller—without a nurse!

I met another mother with a very sick baby. She told me the doctors wanted her to decide whether to keep trying to help the baby or to just turn off the respirator and let her go. I'm glad we never had that kind of choice to make. I didn't really understand it. Matthew had been so sick at some points that the care team hadn't known whether or not he would live, but no one had ever told us we needed to make a choice.

The mother told me she felt that, since God had let her baby live that long, He would not let her die now. That week, there was a big earthquake in Mexico, and a few babies who were still alive were found buried under rubble. The woman on television said, "When the hand of God reaches down in a tragedy and picks out these babies and says, 'Not you', and lets them live, you know there is a special purpose for them."

I don't know, but I was beginning to think there was a special purpose in all their lives, no matter how long or short.

15

Discouragers

I have to be reminded that people are trying to be encouraging. Twice in the month of November, people asked me if it wasn't hard to leave Matthew and go back to work. Of course it was, but we felt we had no choice. We had lived that way his whole life, so we were kind of used to it. The more attentive he became, the more difficult it was to leave him. Then hearing that somehow emphasized how sad it was to have to leave our baby eighty miles from home. I had a few pity parties. I know people had no idea that what they said made me feel worse, but somehow, it did.

One day, we were coming home from the hospital, and stopped to get gas. We saw a man we knew, and he asked Paul how I was doing. Paul told him I was fine and that we had just spent the day at the hospital with Matthew.

The guy replied, "You mean that baby is still alive?!"

I took some pictures to work. In one picture, Matthew was all smiles. I showed it to a coworker, who said, "He looks like he's in so much pain!"

I said, "But he's smiling!"

He said, "I just can't stand to look at him hooked up to all those machines."

I was angry. He wasn't nearly so hooked up to the machines as he had been. He looked happy to me in that picture. That little comment bothered me all day.

One day, a relative was looking at Matthew's pictures and commented that she hated he had the trach collar. Someone had told her that was the most painful thing they had ever been through. Maybe she meant well, but what did she think that comment would do for me?

I was angry again. I'd heard from people who thought it was wrong to save these tiny preemies, and they should be allowed to just die naturally rather than suffer. I saw the point, but I was deeply grateful for the time we'd already had with Matthew. More and more of these babies were thriving.

As I think now about how much these comments bothered me, I guess part of it was that I just couldn't stand to think about him being in pain.

16

Movin' on Up!

A couple of new problems cropped up in November. Matthew had developed kidney stones. The doctors felt this was probably the result of him having been on diuretics for so long. I'd heard horror stories of how painful kidney stones can be. He passed one. It was tiny, but he was only a four-pound baby.

In addition, a vision check found some problem with one of his eyes. The doctors never did explain it (or not so I could understand it), except to say that his vision was probably not going to be affected, and it was a result of being on oxygen for so long.

However, November also brought really good news. At the beginning of the month, Matthew was on the vent only two hours a day, and they were weaning him off that! He was still on oxygen, of course. But off the vent meant a move to the intermediate nursery. We were so excited. Anne told us being off the vent meant beginning the process of going home.

We started hoping for Christmas again. I hinted something about Christmas in front of Anne, and she said, "If you're hoping to have him home for Christmas, you're dreaming."

But I kept dreaming anyway.

On November 6, we moved to intermediate nursery. We loved Anne and would miss her. But Matthew's new primary nurse, Shirley, was just as wonderful.

On November 12, the hospital had some rooms that had been used for nurses in training and now became available for patients' families to use. Paul and I spent Friday night there. When we got up on Saturday morning, we went to breakfast and then headed for the nursery. Paul stopped at the restroom, but I went on in. When I walked in, I glanced in Matthew's corner; he and his bed weren't there. I asked someone where Matthew was. She said, "Didn't anybody tell you?"

I fell apart. She quickly told me he'd some problems breathing and had been moved him back to the NICU temporarily so he could get some help.

Seeing him gone like that had frightened me terribly. I couldn't stop crying. I went out in the hall and met Paul. I tried to tell him as quickly as I could, so he wouldn't get the scare I had. But I could hardly speak. I guess this was what hysterics must feel like. I finally said, "He had to go back to NICU."

When it all happened, no one who was working when we'd visited the night before was there, and the nurses on duty hadn't known we were there and had just tried to call us at home.

When we got to the NICU, one of the nurses saw me. Because I was still crying, she quickly assured me Matthew was OK. They thought he was a little anemic. It turned out he had a bladder infection. I had been so shaken it took a long time that day for me to feel normal.

By November 25, Matthew was back in the intermediate nursery. He was doing well and weighed five pounds. He was the biggest baby in the nursery.

17

Holidays

On Thanksgiving Day, Paul and I spent the morning fixing up Matthew's room at home. We had a balloon theme. Paul had painted the room and put up some shelves. Mama made curtains. The room looked great. All it needed was Matthew.

We had Thanksgiving dinner (lunch) with my family. Matthew had been doing pretty well, and I felt I had a lot to be thankful for. However, I was sad all day. I had cried when Paul prayed at breakfast. I cried when we prayed at dinner. I just couldn't shake it. When we finally went to the hospital, I cried more, and I cried when we left.

Reading this in my journal today, I think, *Well, of course, you cried! Who wouldn't?* But at that time, I felt like crying so much showed lack of faith on my part. Sounds stupid to me now, but that was how I felt.

As he grew, Matthew became more lovable. He also developed a temper. You could see his anger, and sometimes, after a shot or something, he would get really upset and turn blue. One night, he turned blue when nothing else had happened. The care team was a little alarmed about that, and the nurse suggested he might have to go back on the vent for a while. That was a new low point for me. We'd made so much progress; the vent felt like starting over.

On Christmas Morning, we went to the hospital (Santa had to come!). It was a great day. We got plenty of time with Matthew, and he was doing pretty well. That night we went to Mama's. Rodney and Gale had bought Matthew a little rocking chair and brought it out at Mama's. He said, "Next year, we'll see him in this chair!" It made us all cry a little and hope a lot.

By this time, we'd learned all about trach care and how to hold a bottle just right for Matthew to relax enough to eat. On different days, he had different nurses, and some of them were afraid to let us do anything. Some days, when we were working, we'd call the hospital and have trouble getting any information. Sometimes, we'd learn of new developments a few days later. That was frustrating to us. We complained to Shirley about it (although she was always upfront and honest with us).

The big news was that, during this time, the doctor had mentioned Matthew may be sent to our local hospital before he came home. That sounded good to us. But more than anything, we wanted what was best for him, and we kept saying that. Shirley said that, of course, that's what they would do, and our desires would not have more influence than his needs.

18

Whose Baby Is this?

By the New Year, Matthew weighed almost six and a half pounds. He was taking his bottles pretty well. One of the nurses told me on January 7 that this was a special day for Matthew. When I asked why, she said she had been able to get him to drink 18 cc of formula. I thought, *Well, that's nothing new,* but didn't say anything. I did later though. I just had to let her know that I, his mother, had gotten him to drink more than that the day before. I guess I felt competitive with her. This was my baby, and I could do some things for him.

Someone told me they would seriously consider sending Matthew home when his oxygen settings were down to 21 percent. So, I had been watching those numbers. They seemed to stay in the thirties for the longest time. Paul kept telling me not to get my hopes up too soon.

Matthew had passed several kidney stones by this time and still had more. But his kidneys were in good shape, so that was a blessing. Sometimes, his lungs sounded wet, so the doctors gave him Lasix (a diuretic). They thought the Lasix had caused a hernia in his lungs, and for a while, they contemplated surgery for that but then decided he probably had pockets of fluid they could treat with medicine. In January, they also found a stress ulcer in his stomach.

All his life, Matthew had gone from one infection to another it seemed. Shirley told me that could continue for a long time, as he had not really been able to build up immunity.

Matthew was being treated by a physical therapist. He tended to always keep his head turned to the right, so they were trying to help with that. She did hydrotherapy, which he usually enjoyed. Mainly, the therapists just wanted him to get the kind of movement a healthy baby his age would be getting. One afternoon, a little water got into Matthew's trach during hydrotherapy. They got it out very quickly. They thought there would probably be no damage from it. But Shirley said she wanted to be sure to tell me about it, just in case. Water in the lungs can cause pneumonia, which would be very dangerous for someone with all of Matthew's issues.

Feedings were still hit and miss. He wasn't eating as much as they wanted and sometimes refused to eat at all. Shirley told me he might never really learn to take a bottle. But, if we could get him to eat, that wouldn't matter. They had been able to give him a little cereal, but they seemed (to me) to only try that sporadically. They did find he had a reflux problem and thought that was one reason he didn't eat very well.

In spite of all these things, I was mostly optimistic. I felt we were closer to bringing him home than we had ever been.

19

Getting Ready to Go

On February 5, the care team had a big meeting to discuss Matthew. The hospital was actually a medical school, so the team of doctors changed every few months. The meeting was to see where we were, so they could pass the necessary information to the next group of doctors regarding Matthew's particular situation. He was the oldest and biggest baby in the intermediate nursery (seven pounds!). The conclusion from the meeting was that Matthew had reached a point now where it was becoming very important to get him home as soon as possible. He was very aware of his surroundings and needed to be with his family.

They were considering sending him first to our local hospital. They had talked with a pediatrician there who had actually worked in the NICU in Chapel Hill. He felt our hospital could handle a baby like Matthew. That would at least be easier for us. We really just wanted whatever was best for Matthew.

In February, his kidneys were checked for damage from all the kidney stones. There were risks to the procedure, and doing it required our permission. I was a little worried, but the doctors explained everything and said they would call us when they were through and tell us what had happened. Except they didn't. They did the procedure on Thursday. I called that night. His nurse that night didn't know anything about the procedure. I asked if anyone did, and no one there knew. While I was on the phone with the nurse, I asked if his stomach had been upset that day. She said, "Yes, but when he has stomach surgery next week, it will be much better."

I didn't know about any stomach surgery, and she really didn't know what it entailed. All she could tell me was that lots of babies had it, and it helped them.

Times like that were frustrating. The kidney procedure was done on Thursday, and we finally heard from the doctor on Friday. Everything looked OK. He still had stones, but they didn't think there was any kidney damage. Nevertheless, they were having a urologist look at it.

It was Saturday before we would learn about the stomach surgery. They were going to tighten a muscle in his stomach around his esophagus to help the reflux. They were planning to do the surgery the next week, if the surgeon agreed.

On Monday, the urologist reported he had reflux in his kidneys, and Shirley told us he might have surgery for both things at the same time, "since anesthesia is so dangerous for babies with lung disease." Of course, then I wanted to know how dangerous. She just said it was usually the riskiest part of surgery anyway, and it was more so for anyone with heart or lung problems. I felt a little better but not much.

The rest of the week, I kept trying to find out more with no success. Finally, on Saturday, we learned the surgery would be scheduled for the following Thursday (February 28), but they were not going to do any surgery on the kidneys. However, since they were doing stomach surgery, they were going to go ahead and put a feeding tube in his stomach.

Matthew had never been circumcised. Paul mentioned to one of the nurses the possibility of doing that while he was in surgery anyway. Several nurses spoke to us about how unnecessary circumcision was. I didn't care either way, but Paul really wanted him to have it. He guessed that someday Matthew might have limitations or issues. Being the only kid in the gym class who had not been circumcised would make him feel different; it was one difference we could avoid. Someone mentioned that, if we still wanted to do it later, there would be "plenty" more opportunities when he had other surgeries. I could not bring myself to ask what that meant.

We went up early Thursday morning, and everything dragged. We met some of the people assisting in surgery. Matthew had the same anesthesiologist I'd had when he was born. She recognized me and thought I was a nurse. Matthew was happy and smiling and playing before they took him to surgery, so that was good. Paul and I got to be alone with him a little, and we prayed for him. Everyone around us was upbeat, but I was extremely nervous. After they took him into surgery, I went and got his things from the intermediate nursery and kept some of his favorite toys for him to have near him when he woke up. The surgery went well, but we were told by different people where to wait to hear from them. We kept asking and moving, and it seemed forever before we got news that everything had gone fine, and Matthew was doing well. He had to go back to the NICU at first, because he would be on the vent while he recovered. The nurses there were all glad to see him. He was so big that one of the nurses said he looked like a toddler among all those little preemies.

He only stayed in the NICU for two days. When we arrived Saturday morning, he had pulled out a couple of IVs, so now he had one on top of his head with a cup covering it, and they had put socks on his hands, so he wouldn't play with the IV. He seemed to be in pretty good spirits and was off the vent. I wanted so much to help him move back to the intermediate nursery, but they kept putting it off. We finally left that night before they moved him. One great frustration for me was still not being able to do much for him.

On March 10, Matthew was still not cooperating with his feedings. Now that he had the tube, he could be fed that way when he rejected the bottle. I feared he may never want to eat. But I did understand that keeping up his weight was also important.

He still got really upset and could turn blue, but they didn't find anything wrong that would cause that. He still had kidney stones, so it was no wonder he would get upset. He was teething by this time, and I think sometimes that made him cranky. Shirley said he would be the first baby she had cared for who'd gotten teeth! We talked of things like that as if they made him special, and I tried to think of them that way. But in honest moments, I thought of him being the only one because most babies have these milestones at home.

20

We are Going Home

On March 17, Matthew's physical therapist said that, when Matthew got on pretty low oxygen, he would probably go home. At that point, he was still on 38 percent, which was pretty high to me. After getting the feeding tube, he started gaining weight well. He could get all the calories he needed each day, whether he ate or not.

Then they started getting us ready. We learned about his physical therapy. We learned all about trach care. We knew the best way to feed him and how to use the feeding tube. We took a course in infant CPR.

We fixed up his room. We hung a poster over his bed that said, "Where would I be without God's love?" It made us both cry.

By April, the nurses and doctors were talking more and more about us bringing him home. I had always set dates for that. I'd prayed for him to get home by his due date (in October). Then I'd prayed for Christmas, and then Easter. Paul wouldn't do that. He thought we shouldn't get our hopes up. However, at this point, the talk of bringing him home seemed so much like a sure thing that Paul let himself talk about it all the time.

Early in April, the talk was of the likelihood of moving Matthew to our local hospital and then sending him home. One of the doctors there seemed to be making serious plans for his arrival. But then Matthew started running a fever; that meant more tests to see what could be the cause. So, he was put on another round of antibiotics. He still had kidney stones and was still not eating well. But he was close to ten pounds!

On April 20, Dr. Israel called us at home and said, "How do you feel about Matthew coming home?" They were going to find us a nurse to help him at home. They were going to set up oxygen there for him. It was very exciting—and very scary.

That weekend, they let us stay at the hospital and be in charge of all Matthew's care. We got to take him outside for walks. We had done that before, but it was usually with a nurse. This was just our little family, the three of us. While we were outside, the oxygen tank we had ran out of oxygen. So, we took him back up to the nursery. He was fine. Shirley thought this was a good thing. We handled the problem and didn't get overwhelmed, and Matthew did fine without oxygen for over ten minutes.

After reviewing everything again, they planned for another weekend—Mother's Day weekend. This time, Matthew would be staying with us in a room alone all weekend. *Then* on Monday, we would all come home! We were excited. We told everyone we could think of.

There were a lot of things to do to prepare. We had to have the oxygen set up in his room. We had to make his room as clean as possible. We had to contact the electric company to make sure they knew we had a baby on oxygen, so we would be high on the priority list for repairs whenever the electricity went out. We had to contact the rescue department, so they would know how to find us quickly, if we had an emergency. All that was a little scary to me. But the social worker at the hospital did much of the preparation for us. She contacted the doctors at our local hospital so they would know all about Matthew.

Mother's Day weekend was all set. Everything went well. On Saturday, the nurse told us the home nurse we'd thought was coming wasn't available after all. The doctors were considering postponing Matthew's journey home until we could find a nurse. We were upset. Paul asked to see the doctor. I was afraid he might say something to make things worse. But he just told him the tension of going home without a nurse was not nearly so terrible as the tension of finding out we were going to have to wait again. The doctor said they would discuss it. We waited fifteen minutes. It felt like an hour. But they came back and said we could still take him on Monday.

The nurses gave him a little going away party. We were almost giddy, finally able to take our baby home after all these months. Everything went smoothly getting him home. All manner of people wanted to come and see him. We felt a little like some of them were just curious about what he might look like. We did have rules about handwashing and so on before people could see him.

The nurse scare proved to be nothing. On Monday, a wonderful nurse, Bonita, came to our house. The first time we took Matthew to our local doctor, I told him about her. He knew her and said he thought she was the best nurse we could possibly have. And she was wonderful. She came every day for several hours so I could work. All three of us fell in love with her.

The routine of Matthew's care was difficult to get used to. He required midnight medicines and 5:00 a.m. medicines. We had to take care of his trach and suction regularly. His feeding tube had to be taken care of as well. He stayed on a heart and lung monitor that would scream at us every night. It wouldn't stay in place very well if he moved at all. It didn't get easy, but we did it. The first month went well. He had gained a pound when we went back for his first checkup.

He still didn't eat well, but what he didn't eat, we fed him through the feeding tube.

On June 1, I wrote in my journal that he was doing great. That Sunday, we had taken him to my mother's house and then to church that night. Our pastor said, "We're glad to finally have Matthew here with us. Some people say that miracles don't happen, but we have one right here with us tonight."

And we all said, "Amen."

I wrote that, thinking it was a fitting conclusion to the story. I wouldn't have much to journal about now, as Matthew was doing so well—I thought.

21

New Struggles

Pretty soon after my "final journal entry," we had a scare with Matthew. Paul was outside cooking on the grill. Matthew's alarm went off. When I went to check it, he was a little blue. I screamed for Paul. We started CPR and called for a rescue. By the time the rescue came, he was much better, but we sent him on just to make sure everything was OK. He spent a couple of nights in the hospital.

Another time that same month, Matthew started running a fever. We took him to the doctor and again had him admitted to the hospital. The doctor said he was getting ear infections. If they continued, we might have to consider putting tubes in his ears. We came home on his first birthday and had a tiny party that night—just family.

In July, Matthew had what seemed to be something like a seizure. Some of his medications had to be adjusted, and he got better. So this was a short hospital stay. I was suctioning him, and the doctor came in to change his trach. But instead, he asked me to do it and brought in other doctors to watch. One of them told me afterward that I looked just like a doctor doing it. Honestly, Paul would have done better than me under normal circumstances, and I was more nervous than usual because of the audience I had.

On the night of August 7, Matthew was very cranky and had a fever again. We called the doctor, who said to bring him in the next day. He thought he had another ear infection. During the night, the heart monitor alarm went off. I dragged myself into his room and tried to adjust it, but it alarmed again. I called Paul. We couldn't feel his heartbeat. Paul did CPR. I called the rescue. We had seen a little response at first, but now we saw nothing. I wanted to ride in the ambulance, but my request was declined.

After they left, Paul said, "Let's pray."

I was thinking, *No, let's go!*

But he prayed.

After the prayer, he said he felt a peace come over him. I felt no such thing and was upset that he did. I was worried that God must have thought Paul was going to need that peace, and that thought scared me.

We waited forever in the ER. Bonita had been called, and she came and waited with us. Finally, Dr. Nickens came out. We knew as soon as we saw his face that our baby was gone. He shook his head. He was very sweet, saying they'd done all they could. Just like that, it was over. It felt like we had been on a roller coaster for thirteen months, and suddenly it stopped and flung us to the ground—hard.

They let us go inside and hold him. Paul called our families, and everybody came. We stayed in the room with Matthew for a long time. We were all crying, and seeing my parents crying made me even sadder. Even as I write this today, I can see them, and I can still feel that same overwhelming sadness.

The next few days, our house was full of visitors. The door to Matthew's room stayed shut, and the high chair (which he had never actually used) was moved from the kitchen to his room. It felt like family members were trying to hide any reminder there had been a baby in this house.

Initially, I tried to be really spiritual about this loss. I wanted to be a strong Christian, I think. I thought, *Well, if I have to go through this anyway, how can I best honor God?* But when Paul and I were alone in our room, we cried and cried.

We had ordered some developmental toys for Matthew. We would get a new one each month. The afternoon after Matthew died, I walked in the living room where some of our family members were sitting. I asked Mama where Paul was. She said he'd gone to the bedroom. Everyone was somber in the living room. But I just sat down with them. Finally, Mama said, "Go in your room to your husband!"

I had thought maybe he was sleeping. But when I entered the room, I saw he had opened a box the UPS man had brought. It was the new toy for Matthew, and Paul was trying to put it together and crying. Seeing that, I thought my heart would break. Even now, it's such a sad moment to remember.

But the reality was hard for me to face. Our house was suddenly full of plants people had sent. During the night for the rest of that week, I would get up and look around at all the plants to make sure this was really true. I had been so sure God was going to completely heal Matthew, and I knew He had. But that was not what I'd meant.

On the morning of the funeral, Paul got up and went driving around. I guess he just needed time to himself. It was all overwhelming for both of us. For over a year, our main focus had been helping this baby get well, and suddenly all our hope was gone.

The funeral was beautiful. Paul had requested the song, "How Great Thou Art," and our friend Thomas sang it beautifully. It had been Vacation Bible School week at church, and one of the children's classes sang a song called "God Is Very Near" that they had learned at Bible school. After they sang, Mr. Ard said, "Let us pray," and the children sang "Jesus Loves Me." That morning, Paul had said he wished we had asked the children to sing that song, but he only said it to me, and at that point it had seemed too late to ask.

At the cemetery, we saw people from the hospital. Both of Matthew's primary nurses and his lap mom, Ana, along with Dr. Israel and a few other nurses had come. Paul asked them to please come by the house, and they did. We showed them Matthew's room. I felt like I owed them an explanation. They had worked so long to help Matthew live, and now we had lost him. But that was just me. They were kind. Paul told them how grateful we were that Matthew had been able to come home. It was comforting to have them there. They were the people who had loved Matthew as long as our family had. Shirley, Matthew's primary nurse from intermediate care, told me she had been very moved by Matthew's funeral. Anne, his first primary nurse, told us this was one of the only funerals she had ever attended.

I know I was often frustrated with the slowness of information we got sometimes from the hospital. But I also know these were people who were caring for a number of babies all at once, and plans changed as the needs changed. Also, the number of babies who were surviving at younger ages was constantly changing, so the medical community was always learning how best to care for very early preemies. And I also know these were people who loved all these babies and were committed to giving them the best care they could give. The problem with slow information was really just the circumstances they all had to deal with. The fact that a group came when Matthew passed showed their great compassion.

Later that day, my aunt and uncle came from out of town. We all went back to the cemetery to look at the flowers (in our family, that's what you always do). It started raining a little while we were there, and someone said, "Wasn't God good to us, not letting it rain when we were out here during the burial?" I thought, *Why couldn't He have been good enough to keep us from having to bury Matthew at all?* But I pushed such thoughts out of my mind. As a Christian, I didn't think I should have such thoughts as that.

22

West Virginia

Rodney and Gale had made reservations at a lodge in West Virginia for the weekend after the funeral. But now, having already spent so much time away from home (they lived about two hours west of us), they decided they wanted to give the weekend to Paul and me.

I thought that was a kind gift, and it would be good for us to get away. As we were leaving, I remember saying maybe we could go away and get some answers—not that I thought God owed me any answers.

We got to the lodge, and there was a playground in front of our little cabin. We went to the restaurant at the lodge for dinner. It was a crowded restaurant with small round tables. We were right in the middle of the restaurant. There were tables all around us, and all of them had families with babies about the size of Matthew. It probably wasn't really this way, but this is how I remember it. It was hard to eat.

Paul said, "I wonder if I'm just going to go completely crazy."

I knew what he meant. I had no clue how to deal with this. When we went back, children were playing in front of our cabin.

On Sunday, we went to a worship service at the lodge. Only a few people were there. We sang a hymn, "For the Beauty of the Earth." The last time I remembered hearing that song was the Sunday after Matthew was born; it had been sung at the hospital chapel service. So, I cried all the way through this service as well, although now for a very different reason. Hearing the words that had so encouraged me the year before now felt like a mockery.

That afternoon, Paul was going to take a nap. I decided to take a walk. I thought God and I needed a long talk. I felt like He had taken the most precious thing away from me, and now He was rubbing my nose in it. So, on our walk, I told Him that. I told Him I felt He owed me some kind of explanation. Finally, I said, "I'm just so mad with you, God."

As soon as I said it, I realized I was talking to the God who knew all things, was all-wise and all loving. My words sounded almost silly to me. But once they were confessed, they were gone.

I think what happened to me was that God had used all those circumstances to bring me to the point where I could be honest about my feelings and would confess those feelings to Him. I John 1:9 says, "If we confess our sins, He is faithful and just to forgive us our sins and to cleanse us from all unrighteousness." I couldn't help being angry with God and really, until that moment, had not realized it— until I started talking to Him. He helped me see my wrong attitude, so I could confess it. Once I did, He forgave it, *and* he cleaned it up. The anger was gone.

The sorrow was not at all gone. But now I had hope that He would bring me through that as well.

23

Why Now?

My brother, Rodney, said to my dad, "Why now?"

I felt the same way. After all these months, when it had looked so hopeless, and God would come through with a miracle, why had God let it happen now?

Daddy answered with another question, "When would a time ever come when we would not feel this way? When would you say, 'OK, now'?"

Death is always too soon for us. I think my daddy was very wise.

We all dealt with the loss of Matthew in our own way.

Paul's mother started volunteering in the nursery at our local hospital, rocking babies as Ana had done for Matthew.

For the longest time, Paul and I would say, "I've had a Matthew day today."

My Matthew days would be triggered sometimes by running into someone I had not seen in a while, who would ask how Matthew was doing. Such a question would throw me into a tailspin for the whole day. I remember avoiding seeing people who might not know, because I was afraid they would ask about Matthew.

Some Matthew days would come because of something someone said. I understand now that people feel they have to say something, and sometimes what they say comes out wrong. One person said, "Well, he was so sick anyway." For me, that sounded like they were minimizing our loss. I complained to Mr. Ard about it (a frequent habit of mine in those days).

He said, "Well, he was quite sick, and they thought that would be comforting."

I ran into a lady who had a premature son who'd been through a lot but was doing well. She cried when she learned that Matthew had died. So, that whole day became a bad "Matthew day" for me.

Dr. Nickens, one of our pediatricians (and the doctor who had to tell us we'd lost Matthew) asked us to come by his office for a visit. We talked about all that happened, and he assured us that, if Matthew had been in the hospital the night he died, it would not have changed the result. He said it probably would have taken more time to get a doctor to him, and the doctor would have done exactly as we had. He also gave us the book *When Bad Things Happen to Good People*. The book was of some comfort to us, but the visit was even more comforting.

Very gradually, we moved from "Matthew days" to saying we'd had a little Matthew period that day. Eventually, we had Matthew moments. And after a very long time, we had Matthew moments that were very sweet and even somehow comforting.

I know that life would have been simpler and easier if Matthew had never come, but there was never ever a point where I felt it would have been better. A few years after losing Matthew, Paul came across Twila Paris's song "Visitor from Heaven." It captured well what we felt:

A visitor from Heaven
If only for a while
A gift of love to be returned
We think of you and smile.

With aching hearts and empty arms
We send you with a name
It hurts so much to let you go
But we're so glad you came.

24

Another Funeral

Matthew died August 8. Around the end of September, an older lady from our church died. Our pastor, Mr. Ard, wanted to talk to me. He told me that the family had requested I sing "How Great Thou Art" (one of the songs from Matthew's funeral) at her service.

So I said, "No. It's too soon."

He acted surprised. "Will the next one still be too soon, and the one after that, until you never sing again?"

We kept talking about it, until somehow he convinced me I needed to do this.

On the day of the funeral, I was really nervous. I was afraid I might blubber all the way through the song. Some people can sing beautifully and let the tears fall as they sing. I'm not one of those people. So, all day, I prayed about it. I just prayed I would be able to get through it without crying.

But God did way more than answer that prayer.

When I stood up to sing, I felt overwhelmed with joy. I almost wanted to stop singing and tell the family, "I know you have sorrow today. But there really is joy again!"

I didn't do that, but during that song, I knew that joy was not gone from my life. God was still with me. I really could feel His powerful, loving arms around me.

Someone said to me afterwards, "That must have been hard to do."

I told her, "I thought it would be, but it wasn't at all. God was with me, in a way I never imagined."

God didn't have to do that for me. It was pure grace.

25

The Wedding

One sleepless night, I told God that if I could see something of real value coming from Matthew's life, I think I could live with the loss better. Not long after that, we received an invitation to Shirley's wedding.

Shirley had been Matthew's primary nurse in intermediate care. She wasn't a Christian, and we tried to be good examples as Christians around her. We loved her a lot. She was a good nurse and would help us with all our questions.

When her birthday came, I cross-stitched a picture of a little boy and the words, "Jesus and I love you. Love, Matthew." I meant it personally for her, but she put it up for everyone in the nursery, which was okay.

Now she was getting married. As soon as I read the invitation, I remembered my prayer, and I somehow knew we had to go to this wedding. It was a strange feeling, but I knew I would see the answer to my prayer that day.

The wedding was beautiful, and it was clear that this was a

Christian wedding. We went through the receiving line. When we finally were able to see Shirley, I almost knew what she was going to say. She said she had become a Christian and that we planted those first seeds that had started her on that path. I knew God had brought me to this wedding so I could hear this. It was another pure gift from God to me.

Miracles don't always happen the way we expect. But for me, that day was a miracle. I still hear from Shirley occasionally. She has a beautiful Christian family now. How good God is!

Ecclesiastes 11:1 says to cast your "bread upon the waters: for thou shalt find it after many days." Isaiah 55:11 says, "So shall my word be … it shall not return unto me void, but it shall accomplish that which I please." I Corinthians 15:58 tells us that "nothing you do for the Lord is ever wasted" (TLB).

God used our simple efforts to live a life of faith in front of Shirley to accomplish his purpose. We may wait a long time to see the results, and we may never see them. But that day, we saw God's word fulfilled before our eyes. Another gift of grace.

26

December

The first year after losing someone is hardest because of all the "firsts," like the first Christmas. My birthday is December 10. We celebrated and I had a nice sheet cake with sweet, sweet icing on top. The next morning, I was preparing breakfast when Paul came into the kitchen, said something I didn't understand, and fell on the floor. We had experienced times when his blood sugar would bottom out, but this was one of the worst times. He was awake but not making sense.

I saw that birthday cake on the counter, raked my hand across the top of it, and put icing in his mouth. In the meantime, I called his dad, who came over.

By the time he got there, Paul was somewhat coherent and sitting at the table. He kept saying, "I have to get ready to go to work." But we were able to talk him out of it.

That evening, our youth from church went Christmas caroling. One of the visits was the children's part of our local hospital. We were singing out in the halls, and when I looked in the room, all I could think about was when Matthew had stayed there. It had been a tough day already, and I felt overwhelmed and wondered how a person was supposed to be able to handle such things.

Still, we got through it and had a good Christmas. We had other moments throughout the season, but the truth of Christmas still gave us joy.

27

Moving On

Fifteen months after Matthew passed away, Timothy was born and was such a joy to us. I was not afraid to get pregnant again. But now that I'm much older, I wonder that I had the courage. I think, somewhere in the back of my mind, I thought I had messed up the first time, and I wanted to get it right. I know that isn't correct thinking. Having a baby is not a contest or a feat to accomplish. It's a gift. I know plenty of women who have never been able to conceive or carry a baby to term. But honestly, I think a small part was wanting to redeem myself in some way. And we really wanted children.

I had my physical and told my doctor I wanted to have another baby. I wanted to minimize my chances of miscarriage and of preeclampsia. He assured me I had not done anything to make these things happen, but he did prescribe prenatal vitamins.

Getting pregnant was easy, and we were excited, although after all that had happened, we kept it quiet a little while. I knew I was pregnant when a friend from church announced she was pregnant.

This would be her third C-section. My mother-in-law said she was sure the grandmother was worried. I asked, "Why?"

She responded that you can only have two C-sections. But by this time, that wasn't really a concern anymore. Then she said, "If you got pregnant, I'd be so worried."

I didn't say anything.

I started spotting early on in this pregnancy, which scared us to the bone. But when I went to the doctor, everything was fine. On the way home, I was listening to the radio and heard a song I liked. I sat in the driveway for a few minutes to hear it. When I went in the house, Paul met me at the door in tears. He'd been so worried about me, and when I didn't come right in, he was sure I'd had bad news. I hadn't thought about that, or I certainly wouldn't have sat in the car. One bad effect of suffering is we tend to expect the worst.

The doctor did have me quit work at four and a half months and limit my activities. There was an abundance of speculative information on the cause of preeclampsia, and every time I went to the doctor, there was another suggestion from something he had read. I took a baby aspirin, prenatal vitamins, calcium, and iron; rested as instructed; and watched my diet. The doctor said no one really knew the cause, and he was adamant in telling me I had done nothing wrong to bring it about. That was reassuring, as even if the medical community didn't have a consensus on what caused it, other people did. Someone told me to do what my doctor said this time. I said I had before. Someone else told me it was probably because I'd stayed so busy and ate fast food on the run. Those things were hurtful, but I knew they weren't really factual. I trusted what my doctors told me, and I trusted God's sovereignty.

After I became pregnant with Timothy, I started having a lot of dreams about Matthew. I would dream he was alive, and we needed to go to the hospital and find him. I dreamed he was in our bed. I would wake Paul up to tell him to be careful not to roll over on him or to help me find him. (Much later, I was telling a friend about those dreams, and I thought, *Wow, that's so sad!* I felt so sorry for that couple.)

My friend Janice, who had lost her grandfather, told me she kept dreaming about seeing him. She told him (in the dream) that she thought he was dead! He told her he had died, but now he was in heaven and doing fine. I hoped I could have that attitude in my dreams.

During one of those difficult nights, I found this scripture: "When thou liest down, thou shalt not be afraid: yea, thou shalt lie down and thy sleep shall be sweet" (Proverbs 3:24). I claimed this verse for my own, and God took away the bad dreams. If I had trouble sleeping, I would repeat it over and over, and eventually the dreams stopped.

I had feared that having another baby would be a reminder of what we had lost. But this time, it was a different world. Timothy was full term and healthy. Caring for him was so different from caring for Matthew that we never really compared the two. I do think losing Matthew made us particularly grateful for Timothy, and we rejoiced at each phase of his childhood.

We'd wanted to have another baby when Timothy was a little older, but much to my surprise, I became pregnant again before Timothy was even a year old. After getting over the initial shock, we got excited. But it was short-lived. A month after confirming I was pregnant, I began having problems and miscarried within a week. We said we would wait a few months and try again.

In the fall, right around what would have been my due date, Paul complained on Saturday night about being really tired. The next morning, he was making breakfast and dropped an egg. He told me he couldn't use his left hand at all. We dropped Timothy off at Paul's parents' house and went to the ER.

It took a few days to find the problem. The doctor, who had been Paul's doctor for many years, even asked me if Paul had been doing drugs again, but I assured her that he had not. Finally, they told us he'd had a stroke. He recovered well. I could always tell the effects of the stroke by the way his mouth didn't quite turn up right when he smiled, and he had some leftover trouble with his left arm. But I don't think most people would have ever been able to tell. We were very thankful, and soon he was back at work.

28

July 1989

When Timothy was eighteen months old, my phone rang one afternoon. It was the nurse from our family doctor's office. She told me Paul had just been in with chest pains, and now he was on his way to the emergency room. She said they were pretty sure he was having a heart attack.

Paul and his dad had a fence construction business. He and his crew were working on a fence, and they stopped for lunch. He started having pain that he initially thought was indigestion. But the pain was severe and wouldn't go away. They were working at the home of a nurse. She was in the yard and went to speak with him. When she saw him, she asked him if he was okay. He told her what was going on, and she said, "Someone needs to take you to the hospital."

He decided to (drive himself and) go see Dr. Sanford. On the way, he stopped at another house to hang a gate on the fence that was in the back of his truck to save the crew a trip.

By the time I got to the hospital, Paul was in intensive care and in great pain. The nurses only let me go in the room for a few minutes every other hour. So, as I waited between visits, I saw someone I knew but not well. She was asking me about Matthew and if I felt the Lord had helped me get through that. So, I was talking a lot about that. I thought maybe God had sent us here so I could talk to this lady. I was thinking Paul would be fine soon, and we would go home. We were just there for this woman (I'm very good at denial).

The second time I was allowed to go into the ICU, Paul was still in pain, but he'd been given morphine. The third time, he was feeling better, but his speech was so bad I couldn't understand anything he way saying. The morphine, I guess, had finally worked.

The next day, they sent him to Wake Med, which had a heart center. The doctors there did a heart catheterization (checking for blockage) and angioplasty (removing blockage)—all new things to me. It was Friday evening, and we had lots of family there. Timothy was staying with my mom. After the surgery, the doctor came and told us the procedure was successful. Paul was in recovery, and soon we would be able to visit him. But before we could see him, the surgeon came out again and told us they were going to have to do bypass surgery. They had studied the pictures from the previous procedures and found there had been blockage they could not get any other way, and he was still in a lot of pain.

When we went to Paul's room, they were prepping him for surgery. I was crying when I went in.

He said, "I told them you were tough and wouldn't cry."

Some of the prep was very personal. He told the nurse he was going to have to take her out to dinner after this. I was encouraged to see him in good spirits, and I tried to treat it lightly. We were able to pray with him before he went to surgery. Then we just had to wait—all night.

No one had eaten, and it was going to be a long wait. So, we all went to dinner. The hospital cafeteria was closed, so we went out. I could barely eat and was amazed that everyone else could eat and carry on conversations.

Mr. and Mrs. Ard, our pastor and his wife, had been there during the first procedures and left afterward. But while we were waiting during the second surgery, they came walking back into the waiting room. There were family members with us, but still, seeing them come in was a blessing.

When we finally saw Paul in the heart unit the next morning, he was sleeping and attached to multiple leads and hoses and looked terrible. The nurses were kind and said all this was normal. We were allowed to visit about once every three hours for just a few minutes at a time. On Saturday night, other family members went home. Melanie and I stayed at the hospital. Late that night, they said we could go and see Paul. He was mumbling incoherently. The nurse told me she understood he'd had a stroke earlier and then asked if this was his normal way of speaking since the stroke.

I said, "No! I thought this was from anesthesia!"

She said, "No, the anesthesia would have worn off by now."

She called in a neurologist, who told us Paul had apparently had a stroke during or after surgery.

I assumed they meant that, from here on out, this would be all Paul was able to do. I was terribly upset. I didn't know what to do next. I called our pastor. It was late at night, and I asked Mrs. Ard her opinion. Should I call his parents? She said, "If it were my child, I would want to know." Then I talked to Mr. Ard, and he said pretty much the same thing. So I called Paul's parents and woke them up with this bad news and spent a sleepless night.

But the next visit was early the next day, and Paul was much more like himself. He didn't remember much about what had happened but was so much better than I had feared, and he spoke normally. Some friends from church came that afternoon; they were another breath of fresh air. Paul even joked with them a little.

His recovery from the surgery was slow, but the doctors seemed pleased. There was no going back to his old job. Now Paul was going to have to find something new to do.

29

New Life

Years before I met him, Paul had started college to study drafting, but he dropped out after a short time. Now that he could no longer work, he decided to go back to school. His strength was not coming back quickly, and he only took a couple of classes every semester. Going back to school in your thirties can be difficult. But I think it was the best thing for him. It gave him something to work on and a reason to get up every day. He loved it. He wanted to finish and get a job in drafting. I dreamed of that day. I would quit work, stay home, and have another baby or maybe two more.

There was a group of students in all the same classes, and they became friends. All were younger than Paul, but he enjoyed having a group of friends with the same goals. Paul was named after his father, and his family called him Paul Jr. Since his parents went to the same church we did, there were people from church who often called him Paul Jr. as well. One of them was taking a class with him, and on the first day, she said, "Hey, Paul Jr.!" When he told me about it, he was talking about how he needed to correct her about his name at college. I laughed at the picture of this thirty-nine-year-old man being embarrassed in front of his eighteen- or nineteen-year-old fellow students because of being called Paul Jr. instead of Paul.

School was great, but Paul struggled. Drafting was, by that time, much different from when he'd first studied it. It involved computer skills he didn't have and math he had to relearn. Being unable to work and support his family was hard on him. He had a lot of time alone, and that was another adjustment. We often heard people say they couldn't wait until they were old enough to retire and stay home all day. Paul said they wouldn't have felt that way if they had no choice.

His struggle took a toll on both of us. Sometimes, I felt overwhelmed with the new sense of responsibility. I never wanted to talk to Paul about it, because already he felt like he was a burden; I certainly didn't want to reinforce that in any way. I read an article about a caregiver who killed himself after the person he cared for recovered. It made me wonder about support for caregivers. I looked that up on line, but no matter how I phrased it, everything I read was about how to take better care of the person you were caring for. It felt selfish to talk to people about how hard this was for me. I don't think I was ever angry at Paul for being so sick, and I never felt he was a burden. I was grateful we still had him. So, I kept my mouth shut and fluctuated between complaining to God about how hard my life was sometimes and asking Him for strength. And I think that's OK with God. Look at how David complained to God in the Psalms, and there's a whole book in the Bible containing lamentations. I had learned I could be honest with God about my feelings, since He already knew them anyway.

For me, there were two big adjustments. It's an adjustment to suddenly have your husband home all the time. It's also an adjustment when he's no longer bringing home a paycheck. It took two years to start receiving disability for him. The finances did cause a lot of stress for me and sometimes a lot of stress between Paul and me. I thought that, since he had a bad heart, it would be better to try to protect him from worrying about bills. But the problem there was he didn't mind spending a few extra dollars on some toy for Timothy. He didn't realize how hard it was to pay the bills. So, I learned not to pretend things were better than they were. I continued to work full time and took some piano students to supplement, as well as part-time work at church. Still, I felt guilty when he was home alone and guilty if I wasn't at work.

I realized I had tried to hide our money worries from him one day when I told him I was going to close out our savings account to pay some bills. He said, "But that's our money for a rainy day!"

I responded, "Well, it's raining now!"

After the heart surgery, we had a couple of follow-up visits with the doctors, but then we were on our own. Paul did pretty well for about two years. He continued going to college. Then we started noticing his energy level was going down, and he had mild chest pain. Our family doctor sent us to see the heart doctor. Paul had had a second heart attack. They are not always painful, we learned. But we could kind of trace back to about the time we thought it happened.

From that point on, appointments with the heart doctor became a very common thing. Eventually, hospital stays became pretty common too. We became well acquainted with the doctors and nurses at our local emergency room and those at the heart center at Wake.

Timothy and I learned to switch to "hospital mode" very quickly. I kept change (for snacks), a handheld video game, a book to read, and a list of Paul's medicines ready for any sudden ER trips. Today, you could cover most of those things with a phone but not back then. As much as possible, Timothy was in school, scouts, and church and didn't miss a lot of activities. We had a great support team of family members, neighbors, and church friends to help us get him where he needed to be. Timothy learned that hospital mode changed a lot of things in our everyday lives, but he also learned to be flexible when necessary; and I think it gave him a real sense of independence and flexibility that he still has today.

One night, Paul was struggling with chest pain. It was late at night, and I wanted to take him to the ER, but he adamantly refused and finally drifted off to sleep. The next morning, we were to take Timothy to meet the bus to go to Cragmont, our church summer camp. Paul seemed fine that morning. We got Timothy on the bus and waved as they drove away. Then he turned to me and said, "OK. Let's go to the hospital."

In my prayers one night, I told the Lord I desperately wanted to feel I was really doing something for the kingdom of God. I wanted a ministry. Not audibly, but just as clearly, God reminded me that this was my ministry—taking care of Paul and raising Timothy. I still worked full-time and was working at the church as well, so it wasn't as if I had a lot of extra time to do more. But what I had been given to do was important and needed the attention I could give it. Mrs. Ard was our Sunday school teacher and often reminded us, "Whatsoever you do, do it heartily, as to the Lord" (Colossians 3:23). That helped me see the value of whatever I had to do. And I've learned this is always true, for all of us.

Hospitals are always trying new treatments, and several times Paul was able to participate in a study of a particular drug. A tough time came for us when Paul had been offered the chance to try a new medicine for diabetic neuropathy—damage to the nerves that causes severe pain. Paul's was pretty bad in his legs at that point. The study had certain parameters. The severity of the damage had to be within the limits. He really wanted to participate, as his pain had gotten severe and because there would be a payment for participants. He was excited that he could help earn some money.

Paul had to be tested to see if he could participate. The next day, the hospital called me at work and said his neuropathy was too severe and didn't fit the guidelines for the study. I told him that night, and he was really upset. It may seem like a little thing, but when it's the only thing you can do to help your family, it feels like a lot. And, of course, it's never good to find out your problems are way above normal.

30

Mr. Mom

We tried hard to make Timothy's life as normal as possible when he was growing up. There were blessings for him in having his father at home. And there were blessings for Paul in having the opportunity to be there for Timothy.

Timothy never was in day care. He was a healthy child. He was not sick nearly as often as other children we knew his age. But he got hurt a lot. He was always small for his age and wanted to do everything the other boys could do.

Timothy was very attached to his dad. A friend told me, when Timothy wins the Super Bowl, he'll be saying "Hey, Daddy" to the camera instead of Mom. When he got hurt outside, he would run in the house calling, "Daddy!" That was true whether I was at home or not.

When Timothy started kindergarten, he rode the bus to school. The first day he got on the bus, he was confident and brave. I was excited for him, but Paul was crying. He was proud, but now I think he might have been a little sad because, once I went to work, the house would be empty.

But soon Paul was volunteering at Timothy's school. He would read with the kids. It was rewarding for him. He volunteered so much all the kids knew him, and the class gave him a gift at the end of the year. Whenever we would visit the school for night events, kids would rush to say hi to Mr. Paul. I was just known as Timothy's mom (or ignored).

When Timothy got off the bus every afternoon, Daddy was waiting for him. So many kids went home to empty houses or spent the afternoons in day care. Timothy came home and did his homework and played with his friends. I understood what a great benefit it was for a child to have someone to come home to, even though that is rare these days.

31

What Would You Choose?

After the third major heart event, as the doctors liked to say, Dr. Newman talked to me about looking into a heart transplant for Paul. He said he would make an appointment for Paul with transplant doctors. Timothy was about six by now and was with me at the hospital when we discussed that.

As we were driving away from the hospital, Timothy asked what a heart transplant was. I was already overwhelmed by the suggestion from the doctor. So, I tried to explain in as simple terms as I could what that meant. He was quiet for a few minutes, and I was ready to cry, thinking how sad it was that my little boy had to learn about things like this.

Then Timothy said, "Mama, can I ask you another question?"

I said, "Sure." I tried to brace myself for his follow-up question and wondered how hard it would be to answer.

"If you could have any superpower, which one would you choose?"

I laughed, and we had a great discussion about the best superheroes and the best superpowers to have. And I thought, "I guess my kid really is okay."

Another time, we had been to the doctor in Raleigh and were driving home. There was a lot of traffic on the highway, and we were in the left lane but not moving at all. When we got closer, I could see there was an accident up ahead in our lane. The cars ahead of us were changing lanes, and I told Paul he needed to change lanes.

He said, "No, I want to drive in this lane."

I said, "There's a wreck in this lane, and we have to change."

Again, he said, "I want to drive in this lane!"

I knew he must have low blood sugar. I saw a little store on the right of the road and told Paul he needed to stop there and check his blood sugar. He said he didn't need to, so I said I needed to stop at that little store. Somehow, he turned and crossed the other two lanes of traffic and drove up to the store safely. As soon as he turned the car off, I took the key and asked Timothy to go in the store and buy a candy bar and a soda. But he was crying and didn't want to go in by himself, so I told him to stay with his dad and get me if he needed me before I came out. I rushed in and bought a candy bar and soda and brought them back out.

Paul didn't want to eat the candy "because he was diabetic." I got him to drink a little of the soda, but he was mad. I don't know what he was mad about. Low blood sugars do that sometimes, although more often they would make him act silly like a child. He got out of the car and drank a little more and then threw the drink bottle on the ground. I jumped in the driver's seat. In a couple of minutes, he became aware enough to recognize the problem, check his blood sugar, and eat the candy bar. He got in the car and let me drive. Timothy stopped crying, Paul calmed down, and I started driving home.

In a few minutes, Paul said, "That was kind of funny, wasn't it?"

Timothy said, "Oh, yeah, that was hilarious." He's always been witty. Maybe that wit helped him cope with difficult times.

But sometimes, Paul's sickness was really hard on Timothy. One year, a local church had an outdoor Easter pageant. It was very good, and when we got ready to leave, we went to the car. When I got in, Timothy was crying. I thought maybe he was moved by the program. But he said, "Daddy would have liked this. He misses so many things."

All parents know how heartbreaking it is to see your child sad. But I knew nothing to do about it, except pray and comfort him the best I could.

Timothy now tells me that, when he and Paul were home alone together, he was often afraid something would happen, and he wouldn't know what to do. I had no idea he felt that way at the time.

Kids are not always honest about their feelings, particularly if they're not proud of them.

32

Denial

Occasionally, the future would come up in conversation, and Paul would say things like, "If I'm not here by then—"

I would cut him off, saying, "Of course, you'll be here! Don't talk like that."

He even started making suggestions for his funeral, which I really didn't want to talk about. He called me Pollyanna, as I always wanted to say he would be better soon. I always felt like, if we had a plan, everything would be all right. I would just dive into the next plan. Finally, he told me, if we could get some things settled, then we could forget it and not talk about it again. But he really needed to talk about them, so I let him talk about it, and that gave him peace. After that, the subject didn't come up so much.

For a while, I thought our family had had enough loss already; therefore, God wouldn't let anything happen to Paul. Someone told me once about a death in their extended family and how messy the house was when they went to visit. I said, "Lord, please let me have my house pretty neat if I have a death." So, I figured that, as long as the house was a mess, nothing bad would happen. (Yes, I know how stupid this sounds, but it helped justify my poor housework skills.) I kept a journal through Matthew's life but didn't want to do that with Paul—because he was going to be fine. Of course, I had never expected my journal to chronicle Matthew's whole life.

33

Christmas, 1998

This had been a tough year for Paul. He had been in and out of the hospital, and his body was gradually getting weaker. As we started making plans for Christmas, Paul was emphatic about what he wanted us to do. We got in arguments over gifts, decorations, and plans. Finally, he said, "This is my Christmas, and I want it to be right." I had no idea what that meant until he told me he thought this would be his last Christmas. Once he said that, he seemed to calm down a little. Naturally, I assured him it would not be his last Christmas, although I had no way of knowing. That was just my Pollyanna attitude, I suppose.

But Paul did struggle with depression sometimes. Once, we were visiting his cardiologist, and Paul told him he'd been somewhat depressed since his last visit. Dr. Newman said, "If you told me that you were never depressed over your health, I would think you were in denial."

Sometimes, people praise people like me, who smiled and seemed to always stay optimistic. But I think now that sometimes those people may be in denial or may think that, as Christians, they should never show doubt. This is not encouraging to those who doubt and worry. They may feel their spirituality doesn't measure up. We need to be honest with ourselves and with each other. I had great support, but I usually didn't feel it was okay to tell someone when I was discouraged.

34

Pacemaker

After one hospital stay, the doctor noticed that Paul's heart had arrhythmia. They scheduled a cardioversion, which is when they shock the heart to correct the rhythm problem. After the procedure, I met with the doctor, who told me that it hadn't been successful; he would explain it all to both of us when Paul woke up.

They put him in a room, and he was awake and talking, but we hadn't seen the doctor yet. He said he guessed everything went fine. I had to tell him that it hadn't and that soon the doctor would talk with us about it. I hated having to be the one who had to tell him bad news.

When the doctor came, he said we were going to have to get a pacemaker/defibrillator. To prepare for that, they would first do a test to help know how to fix the settings. I think it was something like the stress tests they do now. They would gradually increase the pressure through medicine. I'm telling more than I understand now. Anyway, Paul was sent down for the procedure, and I waited in his room. When he came back, there was blood on his face. During the procedure, he'd bitten his tongue badly, I suppose because of the pain. The nurses had stopped in the hall to clean him up because of the blood, but it was still bleeding when he got back to the room. They got him settled and told me what had happened. When things seemed calm, he started crying. He said, "I will never do this again." The nurse had just gone out and walked back in, thinking something else had happened. He was just glad it was over but still overwhelmed by what he had gone through.

He did get the pacemaker and, a couple of years later, needed to replace it. I remembered how tough that first one had been for him and wondered if he would even consent to it. I know medical procedures change all the time, so maybe the second test was different. Nothing like that happened again.

We had a wonderful nurse through that visit. She prepared lunch for us one day. She wanted us to understand that heart-healthy foods can be good and made the event into a little picnic. People don't know how much simple things like that can mean.

35

EECP

As Paul's heart condition worsened, he was given an opportunity to try something new. It was called enhanced external counter pulsation treatment. They told us he would be the first in the state to try it.

The idea was to put on these pants (he called them Shelby's pants, after the nurse who first recommended them, which became a source of many jokes). Over the pants were cuffs in several places on the legs, and you would hook it up to a machine to push oxygen toward the heart, which was to aid in circulation and help strengthen a weak heart. We felt like it helped some with the pain in his legs and his stamina, at least for a little while.

That June, I won a trip to Myrtle Beach at my job. It was the weekend of our anniversary, and Paul was able to move around much better. We wouldn't have even considered spending the money to take a weekend away to such a nice resort. But God did. Pure grace—again.

36

Stress

I've heard that losing a child puts such a strain on a marriage that many couples divorce. That was not really an issue for Paul and me. I think we both believed so strongly in the sovereignty of God that we never blamed each other for what had happened with Matthew. (Initially I blamed God, and that put a strain on my relationship with Him!)

However, when Paul became sick, it really brought a strain on our relationship, mainly because it brought such a strain on him and on me. He sometimes battled depression. He was frustrated he was unable to provide for his family. He had to deal with fear and with pain. I joked sometimes when he was in the hospital that it was a strain on both of us, but at least they gave him drugs to help. His diabetes had always been very brittle. His blood sugar could go way up and way down in a very short time. High blood sugar makes an unhappy patient. And, of course, anyone who doesn't feel well can be cranky.

It sounds like it was only Paul who was the problem. But I was dealing with the same things, just from a different perspective. I also felt pressured to take care of everything. As Paul's heart got weaker, the medicine bills got bigger because he needed more and more. For a while, we were spending more on medicine than we were on our house payment. I felt often overwhelmed by all of it. It made me impatient and cranky, and I didn't have any physical pain or sickness to blame it on.

For me, guilt was a big factor. I felt guilty if I missed church or work because Paul was sick. I felt guilty if I was with him and couldn't go to church or work. I felt guilty if Timothy had something I couldn't attend because of Paul. I felt guilty doing any of those things when Paul was home alone or in the hospital. I felt really guilty if I did something else just because I wanted to. I finally learned that all I could do was the best I knew, and guilt when there really isn't a choice is not from God. Guilt from God is for things we need to fix or stop doing. Still, I felt guilty no matter which choice I made.

I never hear much about couples in that situation fighting so much. Maybe some of them were stronger than we were. Still, every now and then, God would do something to take the pressure away. Timothy was a delight to both of us. Sometimes, we felt bad that we were unable to do a lot of things other parents were doing for their children. But we worked hard to teach him about Jesus and Christian values, and I think that was the most important thing anyway. Maybe, if we had been wealthier, we would have given him the impression that entertainment and having a lot of stuff were the most important things.

We would have never been able to take Timothy to Disneyworld. But I was asked to go and help on a mission trip to Florida. Timothy came along, and we got to spend a day at Disneyworld. Another time, our friend from scouts invited Timothy and Shawn to go with them to Atlanta with their church group. They paid for the trip as a gift to us.

The business where I worked was owned by my friends Chuck and Marcia, who lived nearby. I'd been looking for a job that could be more flexible because of Paul's illness and frequent doctors' appointments and hospital stays. They had offered me a job, and Marcia told me they knew how our schedules could be, but they would work around what I needed to do. They always made good on that promise. One day, when Paul was in the hospital and very sick, I had planned to go to work in the morning and take Timothy to the hospital after school, as I thought Paul's dad was planning to go to the hospital that morning. But, somehow, our communication was wrong, and he wasn't going. I was sitting at my desk and had been crying a little, thinking of Paul with no one coming that morning.

Marcia walked in and asked me what was wrong. When I told her, she said, "Go! It's fine."

So, I did, gratefully.

Psalm 34:18a says "The Lord is close to the broken hearted" (TLB). In the worst of times, God's grace abounds—if you're paying attention.

37

Drugs

As Paul's health got worse, diabetic neuropathy in his legs became more and more painful and severely limited what he could do.

One of his medical advisors recommended he see a pain management specialist. I imagined this as someone who would teach Paul skills to cope with pain, kind of like a Lamaze teacher does. But he just put him on pain medicine. It was a very strong and very expensive pill. But it did help a little. The next time we went, he said Paul should double the dosage. Now it was helping even more. So, the doctor said double it again. This all happened so gradually I didn't notice how much more Paul was sleeping. I just knew he felt better.

Then we went for the next visit with our cardiologist. He asked a few questions. He looked over Paul's chart. Then he dropped a bomb. "I think what we're dealing with here is drug addiction."

I was stunned. Paul was stunned, and he was furious. He was only doing what the other doctor had told him to do. And for someone who long ago had conquered drug addiction, this was a terrible insult.

We thought, How could he be hooked on drugs when he's just taking what the doctor told him to take?

When we went back to the pain doctor, we told him what the cardiologist had said. He thought it was silly and told us he had people taking many more of these pills than Paul was taking. But after thinking about it (and right after finding out how much these pills were costing us, something I had tried to hide), Paul decided to wean himself off the pain pills. He said it was just like going off of heroin. He did it slowly, but when he got down to only one a day, it was tough. As he lowered the dosage, I noticed he slept less and seemed more alert. I hadn't even realized the side effects of the drugs before that.

A few months later, I was supposed to share a devotion for a women's group at church. The subject was drug addiction. I told Paul about it, mentioning that I didn't think any of these women could relate to drug addiction, unless it was something like pain pills. He said, "Tell them what happened to me!" That had been my plan, but I didn't want to share it unless he felt OK about it. We learned how easily ordinary people can get hooked on painkillers—completely unintentionally. We also learned that you have to stick up for yourself when it comes to your own health care.

A lot of people put doctors on pedestals. I think that was especially true in my parents' generation. It is not always true for me. There have been some wonderful doctors we've dealt with who I love and admire and trust completely. But that is not just because they are doctors. They are men and women who are doctors because they want to help people.

I learned that doctors don't know everything. They may be experts in their own specialties. But they may know very little about other illnesses. Paul went to an eye doctor once who, when he learned Paul had been a diabetic for more than twenty years, said, "I'm surprised you're still living!" We had a couple of experiences with doctors prescribing wrong medicines because they hadn't really checked his charts. Paul saw a doctor who once said that Paul wouldn't be diabetic if he lost weight. We reminded him that Paul was type 1, and weight does not cause that.

Well, enough of that soapbox. Doctors are just people like everyone else. I know Paul lived as long as he did because of some great medical care. I guess my point here would be we need to take an active part in our own medical care and ask questions as needed. Doctors can only know how we're really feeling if we are honest with them, and their advice to us only works if we follow it.

38

Honest Doctor

Dr. Newman was Paul's main cardiologist. We loved him and his assistant, Shelby, dearly. They took time for questions. They were always honest with us. They almost felt like family.

As we went in and out of the hospital, Paul would be very sick going in. But over and over, he would build up his strength and seem better. On good days when I was full of joy, Dr. Newman would tell me, "He is better today, but his condition is still very serious." He'd also remind me that every heart "event" did more damage to his heart. I always told him he liked to rain on my parade. I don't think I so much ignored the warnings, but I was trusting God to make Paul well.

After many such events, we were back again with another one. At the local hospital, they had told us he had another heart attack. We were sent to Raleigh. Paul did get better. Later, I saw Dr. Newman in the cafeteria. I asked him how much more damage this had done to Paul's heart.

He said, "I don't think there could be much more damage to his heart."

Finally, I really listened. I think that day I realized that Paul was really a very sick man. Sometimes, I would get impatient with Paul. I would think, if he would try, he could do more and he would feel better. That day, my attitude changed. I developed a little more compassion, knowing that every effort was a big deal for him.

Paul began falling at home some. We got one of those necklaces ("I've fallen and I can't get up!"). That did prove to be very helpful. By this point, Paul was on oxygen all the time. His legs hurt all the time, and he tired easily.

The doctors talked about heart failure, which to me sounded like you were dead. I finally had to ask how heart failure was different from a heart attack. I understood that heart attacks came from blockage. Heart failure comes from a weakened heart. A bad sign of heart failure would be sudden weight gain. So Paul had to weigh himself daily. He was, of course, on diuretics. The hospital had a program for people with heart failure. Marion—someone else we came to love a lot from the doctor's office—would call Paul every day, asking him his weight. If it went up quickly, she would recommend taking extra diuretics. Sometimes that worked but not always. Whenever he quickly gained ten pounds or more, he would have to go to the hospital to get the fluid off, because the pills wouldn't do it.

Once when Paul was in the hospital, he gained ten pounds overnight. The doctor couldn't believe that could really happen and made the nurse weigh him again. We had seen that happen at home. I wanted to say, "See? It's happening just like we told you." But I also worried what it must mean about Paul's health if this was shocking to a cardiologist.

39

September 2001

Paul and I were on our way to Greenville to see his endocrinologist. The song "Hey Jude" was playing on the radio. In my family, we are big Beatles fans. I said, "I like the part near the end when Paul says 'Hey-ey-ey-ey,' and I sang it for him." (It's just before he says, "Make it Jude," at the very end of the song.) Anyway, we listened to the song, and when we heard that part, Paul said it didn't sound anything like what I was singing. I said, "If I sang that for Melanie, she would know exactly what it was."

Paul's blood pressure was up when we got to the doctor, and he was sent to the ER there. It was a busy place, and we stayed all day. They ran some tests, and then we waited. Paul was feeling pretty good. We found a deck of cards and played rummy on his bed in the ER while we waited, we thought, to be sent home.

Late in the afternoon, the doctor came in to see us and told Paul he was having a heart attack right then. I said, "No, he's not."

But Paul said, "OK."

I figured he knew something I didn't. The doctor said the tests showed that, and they were going into surgery to see if they could put in a stent.

I made some phone calls. Timothy was staying with Paul's dad. I found a vacant recliner in the waiting room and read, prayed, talked, watched TV, and slept a little. At about three in the morning, the doctor came back and said that they had put a stent in, and that was all they could do successfully; Paul would be in recovery until the next morning.

I decided to take the thirty-five-mile trip home so I could take Timothy to school the next morning. I felt like, if Timothy saw me, he would think everything was okay, and he would be okay. Now, I'm wondering if that was foolish of me, but that's what I did.

The next afternoon, Melanie came to the hospital. Paul was still really out of it from the surgery and had hardly spoken. I was stressed and worried about him. When he saw Melanie, he sang, "Hey-ey-ey-ey."

I laughed and said, "Do you know what he's trying to sing?"

"Hey, Jude?" she said.

It was a wonderful little moment for me. Paul was so sick and was trying to lighten my mood. I never hear "Hey Jude" anymore without listening for that part. It always brings a smile.

As Paul was recovering, the doctor was concerned his kidneys weren't functioning as they should. They talked about dialysis if the numbers didn't improve. But in a couple of days, they were normal.

Paul stayed in ICU even when he was better, as there were no beds available for him. But they let me stay with him during the day, so it was more like having a room—with lots of roommates. On September 11, we were watching *Good Morning America* in his room when the newscasters said there had been some kind of explosion at the Twin Towers. We watched as the second plane hit the tower. I went downstairs to get some tea. In the elevator coming back up, a woman was telling everyone about the plane that had crashed, heading for the Pentagon. Back in the room, Paul was shaken up by all this.

Eventually, we saw the doctor, who told us he wasn't ready to go home but might possibly tomorrow. I drove back to Goldsboro to work. No planes were allowed in the air. The only thing on the radio was coverage of what had happened. The drive back was surreal to me, sort of a magnification of what my life already felt like.

Paul's recovery was slow. He couldn't do much and watched a lot of TV, which added to his worry. I was becoming increasingly aware that his overall condition was getting worse all the time. So those were tough days for us both.

Slowly, Paul improved again. I allowed myself to start thinking maybe he would get well enough to go back to school.

40

Homecoming 2001

Every year, the first Sunday in October is homecoming at our church. We have a special service. We have lunch together. We have a memorial service for all who have passed away in the last year. Our women's auxiliary honors a woman from our church each year with a "Life Membership Award."

That year, Paul was determined to go to homecoming. He had not left the house since we got home from the hospital in September. He didn't act like he felt well, but I helped him get ready so he could go.

I learned later why this particular service was so important to Paul. I was honored with the Life Membership Award. I was moved by the honor. I was even more moved when I realized the trouble my husband had gone to so he could be there for me. I felt very loved that day.

Also, that weekend, Paul's son, Shawn, became engaged. Karen was a girl Shawn had met at our church. (This was also where Paul and I had met, my sister and her husband had met, my brother and his wife had met, and my nephew and his wife had met. If you want to get married, come to our church!)

Later, I thought a lot about how many healthy people don't bother with church and how hard Paul was having to work just to be able to get there. I also thought about how little we know about people. It's easy for me to jump in the car and go where I want. But we don't know by just looking at someone else that it may have taken all they could muster to go anywhere. Occasionally, I hear people comment about seeing people who appear healthy using a handicapped parking space. Paul looked pretty healthy for a long time. We are quick to judge when we really have no idea.

The night before Christmas Eve, Paul was feeling really bad. I can't remember why I didn't take him to the hospital, but this time we called for a rescue, and they took him. Several neighbors came over as they were leaving. Elaine, who lived next door, begged us to let her take Timothy and me to the hospital. Her husband was in the air force and was overseas, so she was alone, and she really wanted to do this, so we let her.

We had to sit in the waiting room for a long time. Timothy was upset. He hated to think of his daddy being in the hospital at Christmas. He was embarrassed to cry in front of Elaine and kept asking me to walk around with him. We prayed that Paul would feel better, and a wonderful thing happened. The doctors gave Paul something to ease his chest pain, and it worked! They said to go home. We were all elated. The four of us crowded into the front of Elaine's truck, and we just laughed all the way home.

41

2002

Shawn and Karen were getting married in March. So, our world was busy with wedding preparations. The week before the wedding, Paul had an appointment with the doctor in Greenville. For a couple of days before that, he'd had a bad looking place on his foot. His foot got redder and redder. We figured we could show it to the doctor when we went. By the time we got to Greenville, his whole foot was bright red, so we showed a nurse right away, and they put him in the hospital. It was cellulitis. I'd heard of that but didn't know much about it. We stayed at the hospital all week. Paul had a tooth that was bothering him, and we talked with a dentist there. He told us where we could go and have the tooth checked and fixed and not have to pay.

We got out Friday, so Paul was able to attend the wedding. He was really not well at all, but he got there. I have a family picture from the wedding, and when I look at it now, I realize how sick he really was.

In a few weeks, we made an appointment to see this dentist. We had to wait a while. The dentist told Paul he should go ahead and pull all his teeth. He told him he would start losing teeth one by one and probably lose them all in the next ten years anyway because he had been diabetic so long (*which is not true*). I knew that was wrong, and I also knew what I could not say at that moment. I knew Paul probably didn't have ten years left. I was so shocked at what the dentist had said that I thought there was no way we would do such a thing. But Paul believed him.

I was always of the philosophy that you try to keep all the teeth you can for as long as you can. I had known people who got rid of all their teeth and got false teeth, but I thought that was something you only did if it was absolutely necessary. This would mean putting Paul to sleep for surgery, and I knew he didn't need to have any unnecessary surgery. Our heart doctor agreed with me, but Paul decided to go for it, and I couldn't change his mind. We scheduled the surgery for late August.

42

The Year of Food

After the wedding, Paul did improve a lot. He had become fascinated with some of the shows on the Food Network and started copying their recipes. On the days he felt pretty good, he would try out new recipes. They were completely different from anything I would normally eat. But it was a lot of fun, and it was great that Paul was enthusiastic about something. It was especially nice to come home from work and find supper on the table. All I had to do was sit down and enjoy it (and then wash the dishes. At our house, the unwritten rule was, if Paul cooked, I did the dishes. If I cooked, I did the dishes.)

Most of the time, Timothy helped Paul cook. Sometimes, I would come home, and Paul would have been up too long, and Timothy and I would have to finish preparing the meal. He would sit at the table and instruct us. I told a friend at church about that. He said, "Paul's moved from chef to master chef!"

Usually, my job was to make frequent trips to the grocery store to find some strange spice or strange fruit or vegetable for something Paul wanted to cook.

But Timothy and I remember those days fondly. I think he is a good cook today because of all his daddy taught him, and he learned to try new things.

Still, physically, Paul was not much better. He had a bad sore on his foot that wouldn't heal. Someone from home health came every week to check it and bandage it. He was still falling a lot and getting weaker all the time.

43

Back to the Dentist

By the time of the appointment in August to pull his teeth, Paul had not been at all well. He was weak and didn't really feel like doing much of anything. So I took him on the eighty-mile trip for this appointment. It went fine (except that they really did pull all his teeth!).

Recovery was slow, and of course he had to eat lots of soft stuff. The month of September was slow and tough. Paul did little, and by the end of the month, I was having to check his blood sugar because he was so lethargic. He fell a couple of times. Some days, he just slept all day.

One day, I was home from work on my lunch hour, and a different woman from home health came to check Paul's foot and change the bandage. Paul seemed lost and confused. I had thought at first that he had low blood sugar, but it was normal when we checked it. She asked questions I had to answer, as he was somehow unable to focus on what she was saying. I stayed a little while after she left, and he did seem to be a little better. He called an hour later to tell me the woman had come back. She told him she just wanted to come back and pray for him. We were both so moved by this unexpected act of compassion.

44

Homecoming Again

Homecoming at church was coming up again. On Saturday night, I was preparing some of the food I would take the next morning for lunch at church. I was supposed to teach Sunday school also. Paul asked, pleaded really, that I not go to Sunday school and stay with him until time to go to church. So, I called Mrs. Ard, our pastor's wife, and asked if she would teach in my place. She agreed and then asked if she could talk with Paul. He was sitting on the side of the bed as they talked and was crying while she was talking. He bowed his head, so I knew she was praying with him.

After they hung up, he said, "Did you notice me coming up off of the bed?"

I had not seen that.

He said, "Mrs. Ard prayed that Jesus would hold me in his arms, and when she said that, it felt just like He picked me up like a baby and was holding me."

By now, we were both crying. I thought of the verse, "The

eternal God is thy refuge, and underneath are the everlasting arms" (Deuteronomy 33:27b).

Paul slept peacefully that night. I was grateful for what God had done for him. Nothing like this ever happened to me. Still, I wondered why Paul needed this at this time.

On Sunday morning, we had breakfast. Paul and Timothy were still at the table, and I went to get a shower. I told Paul, "Please don't try to leave the table without Timothy or me here to help you."

But he did. I heard him hit the floor while I was in the shower. When I got to the kitchen, he was lying on the floor, and Timothy was trying to help him get up. Paul was a pretty big guy, and Timothy was a small kid, even though he was fourteen. But even after I tried to help, we couldn't get him up, so I called rescue to come and help us. Timothy told Paul he thought he should go on to the hospital when they came. Before they came, Paul asked me if I had told Timothy to say that. I hadn't, but I told him I thought Timothy was right. So, he agreed to go. I remember wondering as the ambulance left that day if Paul would come home again. But I quickly pushed that thought out of my head.

I was the pianist at church, and the choir had learned a new song for homecoming. It was a little tricky to play. I knew no one else had even practiced playing it, and the choir would probably need to find a different song. I felt bad about that. But then I thought, if God had thought this song was so important, He could have made a way. I dropped Timothy off at church after the rescue left with Paul and met them at the hospital.

Of course, Paul was hooked up to IVs and oxygen. They let me stay in the little room in the ER with him, and others could come one at a time. We weren't there long before we learned we had to go to Wake. Mama and Daddy came and wanted to come back there and see Paul before we had to leave. I asked the nurse, and she said one of them could come. I told her we couldn't separate them, that they were joined at the hip. They were so close it seemed hard to imagine even asking that only one come. The nurse allowed it—but for only a few minutes. When they got there, I was glad they couldn't stay long, because they looked at Paul so sadly. I tried to make light conversation, but they stayed serious. I hoped Paul wouldn't notice. If he did, he didn't say anything.

Up at Wake, we had a routine that had become all too familiar. As with every hospital visit, the first thing we had to do was answer lots of questions. I had long ago learned to carry a list of medications with me for the next doctor or hospital. They asked Paul what they should do if he stopped breathing. Would he want to be revived?

He said what he always said, "Sure! Do whatever you can!"

The first project was to get fluid off. This meant getting stronger fluid medicine through IVs until he got back to his normal weight. That never took too long, and I thought maybe this was going to be a quick fix.

After staying there about two weeks, Paul had another heart "event." After that, he was in ICU and sleeping all the time. His kidney function was down. We had to meet with a group of doctors we didn't know. They said he needed dialysis, but they didn't recommend it. They wanted me to sign a DNR (do not resuscitate). I didn't want to do that. We asked lots of questions. I asked if we could wait and see if the kidney function improved. That had happened before. They said it wouldn't.

Timothy said, "If he gets better—"

And one of the doctors said, "He will not get any better."

Finally, we agreed to think about what they had said and talk to them the next day. Paul's dad did not want us to do dialysis. I didn't know what to do about that, but I did know I wasn't going to sign a DNR. I have learned since then that there are many times when the best thing to do is to sign it, but at that time, I wasn't ready to do it.

The next day, Paul's kidney function improved. He gradually got better and was alert and talking. Someone from physical therapy would come and try to get him walking, but he was too weak to walk.

Sometimes, all he could do was stand up. The first time a therapist tried to help him walk, he couldn't even stay up. Apparently, I was looking sadly at him. The therapist snapped his fingers, and when I glanced at him, he gave me a mean look. I knew immediately that my expression was not encouraging, and I made sure to try not to do that again.

Another morning, when the therapists tried to help him walk, he told them he was sure he would be able to take a few steps. But he couldn't. As they were getting ready to leave, though, he said, "OK, tomorrow will be the day. And if not tomorrow, then the next day. We'll just keep working on it!"

I was so proud of him at that moment. It could have been so easy to give up. And, honestly, he had moments when he felt like that, which made his determination and upbeat attitude so moving to me.

He had to have a temporary trach put in at one point. Eventually, he was being treated by a doctor for his heart, a doctor for his breathing, a doctor for his swallowing, a doctor for his diabetes, and physical and occupational therapists. (Occupational therapy is for fine motor skills, we learned. I thought it sounded like they were going to find him a job.)

Things continued in something of a cycle. He would get a little better and then suddenly get a lot worse. He was in and out of intensive care. But he was not getting well enough to walk or to consider getting out of the hospital. Timothy's birthday came. I let him have a slumber party at home. The next morning, a friend of mine was having a yard sale. So, I took all these boys to yard sales. They bought cars made for little kids to ride in and broken go-carts to ride. I left them at home and went to the hospital. These fifteen-year-old boys were laughing all the way back home, all excited over their new toys, which they broke the same day.

For a hundred dollars, I bought my friend's living room suite. It was newer than what I had and in better shape. I didn't have a hundred dollars, but she said she was going to have another yard sale the following Saturday. I could bring my living room furniture, and she would sell it. Then I could deduct what she got from my stuff and pay the rest. So we agreed. After her second yard sale, she brought me ten dollars from what she'd sold of mine (after taking out the hundred dollars I owed her). I love a bargain.

On the first Saturday in December, our custom was to attend the pancake breakfast at the Boys and Girls Club, go to the Christmas parade, and find and put up a Christmas tree (a real tree as God intended). But we knew that hospital mode trumped customs sometimes, and so this year was different. Timothy's friend, Tanner, came and spent the night with Timothy. The next morning, the three of us went to the pancake breakfast. Tanner asked me about three times when I was leaving for the hospital. I thought, *He's ready for me to take him home.* I took both boys to Tanner's house and went to the hospital.

That night, I came home from the hospital, and the outside of my house was decorated for Christmas. Timothy and Tanner, along with Tanner's dad, Dennis (probably mostly Dennis), had done it while I was gone. What a great gift.

My birthday came the next week. Paul wasn't really aware of too much at that time, so he never thought of it.

Christmas came. Paul was aware of that. He hated that he was in the hospital at Christmas. We did too. But since Paul had been in the hospital since the first of October, we were kind of used to it. We went up Christmas day and opened presents. We worked hard to make it feel as normal as possible. I handed Paul a gift to give Timothy. Paul's dad had bought him a gift for me. Paul apologized that we had to come to the hospital on Christmas Day.

Timothy said, "I wouldn't want to be anywhere else."

Paul said, "I would."

We had gotten into something of a routine. Most days, I drove Timothy to school and then headed for the hospital (about an hour away). I would leave after I got a chance to talk with the doctor unless something else was going on. Then I would work in the afternoon. One or two days a week, I worked mornings, and Timothy and I went to the hospital after school. My bosses and coworkers were *great* about my schedule. They pretty much let me do what I needed to do.

I kind of got used to the routine and even learned there were some perks when you stay in the hospital so long. I knew my way all around that big hospital. I got an employee discount in the cafeteria. I knew the schedule and knew what days my favorite foods were served. I got to know a lot of people. On my birthday, the woman from the financial office contacted me to wish me a happy birthday. One of the therapists gave Paul a haircut. Little things like that mean a lot when you are going through something like this.

Melanie and Johnny were at the hospital one weekend when Paul was in ICU. I had been sleeping in the waiting room for a couple of nights. The hospital had a hotel attached for family members, but it wasn't free—or cheap. So, I never used it. Before they went home, they bought me a night in the hotel. Sleeping in a bed and taking a shower were such luxuries. Now that I realize I had not been able to take showers, maybe that's why they did it! No, it was just a very thoughtful gift, and it meant a lot.

During those months, we were in and out of ICU. Most ICUs have strict visiting times, like maybe fifteen minutes every hour. But if there is something going on in the unit, like someone moving in or out, they postpone the visiting times for everyone. A big hospital like Wake had several different ICUs. Some just had curtains around the beds, and some had little rooms. Sometimes, when things were calm in the ICU, and the nurse felt OK about it, I could spend all my time in the room with Paul. There were other days when I had to sit in the waiting room until visiting time. I especially tried to be around to see the doctor whenever he made his rounds.

One of Paul's nurses in ICU was very strict. A couple from our church came by. I was talking with them in the hall when Paul's nurse came out. She saw them and exclaimed, "They can't go back there to see him!"

They said they'd just stopped by and didn't expect her to let them see him. We laughed about that.

Even though the routine became familiar, there were tough moments. I knew this was supposed to be a temporary time. People aren't supposed to spend months in a hospital. It was always an emotional roller coaster. Things were better, and then *bam*! Along would come a new problem to deal with. Occasionally, I would have really dark thoughts. Paul had a handicapped parking pass. It was a plastic thing you hang in your car on the rearview mirror. One morning, I was getting into the car as I was leaving the hospital. It broke in half. I first thought about trying to replace it, although I never used it unless Paul was in the car (not that I wasn't tempted). Anyway, I thought I may never need to replace it. But, of course, I pushed that thought right out of my mind.

One of the times when Paul seemed really sick, the doctor approached me again about signing the DNR. I told him what Paul had said when he went into the hospital. He said, "But he wouldn't have wanted to live like this. I think sometimes families are thinking of themselves and wanting to keep their loved one around no matter what condition he is in."

That hurt me. I certainly didn't want Paul to stay in the shape he was in right then. But I also wanted to give him the very best shot we could. And I knew that, had I signed the DNR a few months earlier, Paul would not have been there at all, and we'd had some good times.

A few years ago, someone close to me had a spouse who was dying. I mentioned that I didn't know what that must feel like. They said, "What do you mean? You went through the same thing!" But I really didn't think of Paul as dying, even though I knew he was really sick. I was concentrating on making him well. Whatever hurdle we came to, I just looked for the next plan to fix it. Maybe it was denial, but I think it was just dealing with life as it came.

The Sunday after Christmas, Timothy and I were on our way to the hospital after church when our car broke down on the highway. We knew a mechanic who had a shop nearer home, so we had the car towed there. He worked on the car on Monday and called to say it was ready. I said I'd pick it up Tuesday morning. When I went to pick it up, the mechanic asked how the car was driving.

"I just came to pick it up," I told him. "I haven't even seen it yet."

He was shocked and realized what had happened. The person I had spoken with the day before had not relayed the message, so my keys had been left in the car, and someone had stolen it.

I went back home and called my insurance company to ask what I needed to do. Then I went to work. I remember saying to my coworkers, "Don't talk to me! I'm a jinx. I'll bring you bad luck!" I didn't really believe that, but it sure felt that way.

But at the same time, some pretty exciting news was brewing. The first was that Shawn and Karen were expecting a baby! And Paul had encouraging news. His doctor had talked to him about going to rehab. The people from the center had visited him and told him about the place. It wasn't any closer to our home, but it was certainly a step up. He said it would be like a small apartment, and the therapists would do a lot of physical therapy to help him get enough strength to walk again. He hadn't walked any since entering the hospital in October. He was pretty excited, telling me he was going to get a "bachelor pad like Howard Sprague." I know nobody but me would have understood that. It was a reference to an old *Andy Griffith Show* episode, in which Andy's friend Howard got a real hip apartment (hip for him), and he called it his bachelor pad. It was a silly show and a silly reference, and I was glad we sort of had an inside joke. Normal husband and wife communication was rare for us in those days.

In just a few days, they moved him there. We were ecstatic. Of course, it wasn't much of a bachelor pad. It was really a nursing home with a rehab section, but still we were happy to be making some kind of progress. The second day there, a man was going from room to room with a guitar singing for the residents. He sang "Amazing Grace" for Paul, who was so moved he called me at work and made the guy sing it again (all four verses!) while I listened on the phone. Paul was crying, and it was very pretty. What an impact such a simple thing can have on a person.

But the progress was short-lived. On Friday, someone called to tell me Paul had a blood clot in his leg and was going to have to go back to Wake. I asked if they had told him, and they had. She said, "He's OK with it. He cried a little." I was almost as sad that I had not been with him when they'd told him as I was about this new setback.

On Saturday, we had lunch with Shawn and Karen for her birthday. Then we went to the nursing home. By the time we got there, it was nearly time to transport Paul. But he was in very good spirits, making jokes with the nurses. We were only there a few minutes before they left.

The plan was to do some kind of surgical procedure that would block the clot from moving up. I'd originally been told it would be done on Monday. But by the time he was at Wake, he had a lot of fluid, and that needed to be taken care of first.

At the hospital on Monday, Paul was confused. Although Timothy was at school, Paul told me he'd promised Timothy he would help him with some homework and that I needed to go out to the hall to get the papers for him. I tried to change the subject, but he was so insistent I finally told him there were no papers to get. I said, "Do you remember how sometimes medicine can make it hard to think correctly?"

He said, "Yes, but this is what I promised Timothy!" He was getting really upset with me.

I told him he knew I wouldn't lie about something like this, and I was telling him the truth. Then he believed me. I was glad he knew he could trust me in spite of his confusion. We turned the TV on. *Family Feud* (one of Paul's favorites) was on, and I tried to get him to watch it, but he said he had never seen that show before. I don't know what had made him so confused.

The next day, Paul became very sick from the fluid buildup (congestive heart failure) and was put in ICU. I worked in the morning. After school, Timothy and I went to the hospital. We had to wait a long time to even see him. I thought he looked terrible after the first visit. He was not aware of anything and didn't respond to anything we said. We waited for the second chance that night to visit. This time, the nurse had me sign a paper permitting them to do dialysis the next morning. Kidney function was down again. I said, "What if I wait until tomorrow to sign it?" (I was thinking his kidneys might improve, as had happened before).

She answered, "Then he'll die."

So, of course, I signed. It had been a hundred days since Paul had been home.

When we went home, we called family members. I wanted them to be aware that he was really sick. Timothy went to bed, and I rested on the couch a little and fell asleep there.

A little after midnight, the phone rang. It was the hospital. They told me Paul had died. I was so stunned. I said, "Are you sure?"

She asked if we wanted to come that night. I said no and had to give her the name of the funeral home we wanted to use. I couldn't believe it. I was crying so hard I guess I woke Timothy up, or maybe I called him. We had enough sense to realize we had to make calls.

Then the phone rang again. It was the hospital. I thought, *Maybe it was a mistake.*

But they just wanted to know what to do with Paul's things that were there. It wasn't much, so I just said I didn't want it. I think Timothy was a little more composed than I was, at first. I called Paul's dad and my sister. Shawn's mother had died less than a year before, and I was talking about how I hated to tell him. Then Timothy said he would call Shawn. It was after that call that Timothy kind of fell apart. He told me later that, once he said it out loud to Shawn, the reality hit him. They prayed together over the phone. I felt bad that I had put such a burden on him to call his brother, but I'm not sure how I would have handled the whole thing alone.

Much of that night is a blur to me now. I kept thinking, *Why couldn't they come up with a plan to fix what was wrong?* There was always another plan. Could it really be true?

Even the next day, when we went to the funeral home to see him, I thought maybe they'd find out it was a mistake. I guess I really couldn't believe it until I saw him. I don't know why I'm that way, but I was the same way with Matthew.

The next days were a whirlwind of visitors and decisions. We had visitation at the funeral home the night before the funeral. Lots of people came, some making us cry and some making us laugh. One of the teenagers Paul had taught in Sunday school (now an adult) brought a card and said to me, "I want to invest in your life, as Paul invested in mine." Later, I opened the card, and there was money in it. I remember during a moment to myself going over to look at Paul. I touched his hair, perfect and soft as always. I wanted to do that to remember when I would wonder if this really had happened. Paul's nephew came and joined me pretty quickly.

I thought it was very sweet when a group of Timothy's friends from school came. They pulled chairs together and all talked for a long time.

I planned the funeral just as Paul had requested. We had the song "The Old Rugged Cross." It had meant so much to him when he was first a Christian. My sister-in-law, Gale, and my brother-in-law, Johnny, played the piano and organ, and our friend Rick sang. Rick and Paul had worked together with Cub Scouts. Shawn spoke for the family, and then Mr. Ard spoke. All I remember that he said was, "No more trips back to Raleigh." I remember thinking, *What will I do now?*

Later, people asked me why I didn't have this or that song. I told them this was what Paul had wanted. (I wanted to ask why they would say that to me after it was over, but I didn't.) People do say the strangest things sometimes. Someone asked me if I was relieved. Such a thought had never entered my mind. One woman told me she had been looking forward to Paul's funeral, as she was expecting a particular singer who she liked.

Timothy was fine. People kept asking him how he was doing, and he always said he was fine. He told me he wished people would quit asking because he was fine. He even said that the night of the visitation. *Too fine*, I thought. Someone said to him that now he was the man in the family. I said, "No, he's the teenager in the family." I didn't want him to feel that kind of pressure.

In addition to everything else, my stolen car was found, totaled. So, I had to buy a new car. At the bank, someone referred to me as a widow. Of course, I knew I was a widow, but somehow that was shocking to hear.

45

What Do I Do Now?

I was telling a widowed friend about that and about how, after Paul died, I thought, *What do I do now?* She said her thought was, *Who am I now?*

I heard a speaker talking about a tragedy in her life. She told her pastor she didn't know how she would ever get over it. He said, "You don't have to get over it. Don't put that kind of pressure on yourself. You just have to get through it." That was great wisdom for me.

Timothy and I gradually developed a "new normal." I felt guilty about anything fun I would do. Sometimes, in the past years, there would be opportunities to take trips. But if they were overnight, I just didn't go. Now there was a trip our church was taking, and I realized I could go. I had a good time but felt guilty. *Paul had to die for me to be able to take this trip*, I thought.

About two weeks after Paul died, a friend of ours lost her husband. They were close to our age. About a month later, she came by our office, and she and I talked. We cried and talked about some of the strange feelings we had. She told me she had been going to grief support at the funeral home and encouraged me to go. When Matthew died, someone had told us about grief support groups, but I'd thought of them as pity parties (I don't think that anymore). But after Paul died, I considered it. The person I most wanted to talk to about it was the one who was gone.

I thought I would go because I was concerned about Timothy not dealing with his grief. He was still doing fine and wanted people to quit asking him. When I got there, I cried the whole time. I talked about Timothy. Reverend Sauls, who was in charge of the group, told us that grief is hard work, and young people don't want to do it, but that eventually, Timothy would come around. I also talked about guilt. He assured us that everyone deals with grief in their own way and in their own time. But it's not fair to compare how badly you feel with how much you loved your spouse. That was the big one for me. I felt bad about feeling good. There were other people there with sad stories to tell, and I cried for all of them. But grief support was very good for me. I went for almost a year.

I would sometimes try to get Timothy to talk about his feelings. We ate at the kitchen table where we had always eaten, and sometimes I would talk a little about Paul. He started asking if we could have dinner in the living room and watch TV. I didn't like that idea, but I thought maybe it was because I talked too much about Paul. But he finally told me how sad it was to eat at the table in our regular seats with Paul's empty chair there. I rearranged the setup so it could be a table for just two. I also began to appreciate that Paul's favorite chair was no longer in our living room. Paul had never seen the living room furniture I'd bought, so it was never a reminder.

I slept on Paul's side of the bed and have since heard other widows who said the same thing. I was pretty used to sleeping alone after such a long hospital stay. But even so, sometimes I woke up and remembered he wasn't there, and this time he wouldn't be coming back.

Paul and Timothy had been close. I had worried about his response to losing his dad. His grades suffered a little, I think because of Paul, and because of no one being there when he got home from school, and from just being a teenager. Even after Timothy was in college, one day he told me, whenever he cut himself shaving, he thought how unfair that he didn't have his dad to teach him how. I reminded him—again—that he'd had more real time with his dad than most kids do. I mentioned that to a couple of friends who, although they had husbands around, the wives still taught their sons to shave.

Not long ago, Timothy told me he used to tell his dad, "I want to be just like you when I grow up."

Paul always responded, "I want you to be better than me."

I thought, what a great wish to have for your children. Many want their kids to have the things they didn't get or have an easier life than they did, but I think Paul was more concerned about the kind of person Timothy would be.

A lot of people knew how sick Paul had been. Several times after he passed, I ran into people who would ask me how he was doing. I would be upset, although I wouldn't let them know, of course. I started trying to avoid situations where I might run into someone who didn't know Paul had died, just as I had when Matthew died. I told Timothy that, and he said he was glad when people asked; it meant people remembered his dad. So, I tried to change my perspective.

I threw lots of energy into raising Timothy. The milestones in Timothy's high school years were a little bittersweet. I wished Paul could see what a fine young man he was becoming. Timothy and I went to a jewelry store to buy his class ring, and I wished Paul could have been there with us. As we were leaving, the lady who worked there said, "Bring your husband back and get him to buy you something nice!" I couldn't answer, and we just kept going out the door.

Karen had Isabel in July, and we loved her so. Sometimes I thought about how sad it was that Paul had never gotten to see her. She was born at the hospital where Paul had spent so much time and where he'd passed away. We, of course, were in a different section waiting for the birth, so it was not a problem for me. I wanted to go to the big ICU waiting room and see if I could see anyone I knew.

When we approached the room, Timothy said, "I can't," and went back to the other waiting room. I felt almost that I needed to stay, and I did feel a sense of closure. I was able to see a few nurses and Dr. Newman and Shelby and talk to them. And of course, they were gracious. Just like when we lost Matthew, I somehow felt it was a failure that was my fault, and I felt bad for those who had spent so much time taking care of him. I know that feeling is not logical, but often feelings are not. That did pass eventually. Just like with Matthew, I did battle dreams that Paul was still alive. But this time, I knew God could pull me through.

Christmas came, and we had a great time, I thought. On Christmas day, Timothy and his girlfriend got some balloons and let them go. They said they were sending them to Paul. I was in the living room at the time, when Timothy suddenly burst in the door, sobbing. He said he was missing his dad. I said, "But haven't we had a good Christmas?"

He said, "Yes, and Daddy loved Christmas!"

It had almost been a year. I think this was the beginning of healing for him. He was finally facing his grief.

Since then, there have been losses of extended family members (and close as well). I thought about how Paul didn't have to grieve over those things. I stayed very busy. I was very involved at church. I was working full-time, and soon I had the chance to start writing Sunday school literature, which was a great boost for me. We did kind of reach that "new normal." Timothy says I had a midlife crisis. We took up all our carpet and painted almost every room in the house (different colors). I don't think it was a midlife crisis so much. It was just the first time I had the opportunity and time and funds to do anything like that. And since I wasn't married, I could pick any colors I wanted! Timothy's girlfriend at that time said my house looked like a bag of skittles.

When Timothy started thinking about college, I knew I didn't want him to feel he needed to stay close to look after me. He believed me and went to UNCG—two hours away. I was mentally prepared for him leaving, I thought. But once the house was really empty, I grieved all over again. I had thought of myself as needing to be there for Timothy after Paul died, but I think it may be more that Timothy was there for me. I think he and I have a unique relationship. I was talking to another mother who was raising a son by herself, and she said she felt like it had always been her and her son against the world. I get that. When he left for college, it was the first time in my whole life that I'd ever lived alone. I thought about times when Paul would be home alone most of the day, and I felt sad—and guilty.

I went to White Lake with a couple of my college friends. I came back really late on Saturday night. I remember driving home, thinking that no one was there waiting for me. Nobody would know or care if I came home in the middle of the night. For a minute, I felt sad. Then I thought, *I can stay out all night if I want to! Anytime!*

I didn't, though. I went on home. But I tried to look at things with that perspective.

46

Does Time Really Heal All Wounds?

A year after losing Matthew, I wrote in my journal, "Matthew has been gone for a year now. I couldn't have imagined that it could still hurt as much as it does today. Even now, we both have moments when the pain is as real as it was when we first lost him. And even now, I have moments when I can hardly believe it's true."

For this book, I have been reading my journal again. It is full of numbers that I can't really understand any more—blood gasses, oxygen levels, and other numbers we followed so carefully. Some parts make my heart ache just as it did then. Sometimes, I'm almost detached from the sad parts, and I think how sad this was for this young couple. Some parts are so sad I can't imagine how we got through it. But the journal is full of moments when God made His presence known to us. The scripture came alive. Corrie ten Boom wrote that, in the concentration camp, the word of God was so real to her that sometimes she wanted to touch the pages to make sure the ink was dry.[1] I know my experience would never compare to hers, but I think I learned a little bit about what she meant.

For the longest time, I was in denial about Paul's condition, I think. I sort of thought that a good God wouldn't let me lose Paul after having lost Matthew. It would just be too much. So, I just kept expecting that he would get better.

One day, during the last long hospital stay, my friend Marcia and I were talking. She said she'd told her sons we may have to say goodbye to Mr. Paul sometime because he was so sick. She said to me, "Of course, I know you and Timothy have had that conversation."

I didn't say anything, but we hadn't.

One Sunday, Timothy and I were at the hospital, and we went into the small chapel there. We did talk honestly about the pain and limitations Paul had been struggling with for a long time. We discussed the possibility of it never getting get better, what Paul would want and what would we want for him. I think that was the only time I really acknowledged that he might die and that it would be a blessing for him.

However, I went right back to my job of helping him get better. For me, denial is hard to shake.

---

[1] Corrie ten Boom, *The Hiding Place* (New York: Bantam Books, 1971), 195.

47

June 26, 2008, Blog

Author's note: The following blog was written on Matthew's twenty-fifth birthday. I wanted so much for someone to remember that. But if they did, no one mentioned it to me, maybe because it would make me sad if I hadn't thought about it.

I wrote the following in my blog:

> Twenty-five years ago today, I had my first baby, a tiny one pound, ten ounce boy named Matthew. He was sixteen weeks early. He lived for thirteen months. That was a joyful and heartbreaking year for us. We got through hurdle after hurdle and rejoiced with each new thing. We were so stunned when we lost him.
>
> Someone asked me recently what do grieving mothers most need to hear. I think they need to know that there will be joy in their lives again. I remember thinking after Matthew was gone that joy went with

him. He left a big hole in my heart. But because the hole was so big, it took a lot a joy to fill it, but God really did that.

I've learned there is no such thing as "getting over it." Always, the ones you have lost are part of you. And that's a good thing. There is always that hole. But eventually, you remember and are thankful you had the opportunity to have that child—no matter how short the time was.

I lost my husband Paul in 2003. Our twenty-ninth anniversary is this week too. This morning at church, we sang "Amazing Grace." The third verse suddenly struck me: "Through many dangers, toils, and snares I have already come." I thought, *I have been through many terrible things* (but now I would add, *just like everyone else*).

"Tis grace hath brought me safe thus far. And grace will lead me home."

I was moved to tears, knowing that I am well and happy—all because of the amazing grace of God!

My pastor asked me tonight, "What would you say to twenty-five-year-old Matthew if you could? What would you say to Paul now?"

I've been thinking a little about that. I think I would tell Paul how great Timothy has turned out, and that he would be so proud. It's harder with Matthew. I think I would tell him I still love him, and I understand that he couldn't stay here, and I'm glad for heaven.

I've had a good life here so far, and he was an important part of making it good.

48

Scars

To be honest, I think we all have scars from what we've been through. I still worry too much and sometimes fear the worst. I think I should be more empathetic, and I am if you have someone in your life who is extremely ill. But for other things, not so much. I tend to mentally minimize other people's concerns if they strike me as "not so bad" or fixable. Of course, the stupid little things I worry about are still huge!

Knowing this about myself, I try to keep all that in check. I know that if something is keeping you up at night, it would not help for me to minimize it. And if it concerns you or me, it concerns God. So, I am trying to have his heart for other people.

I know there are many people who have much greater losses than I have had. It is easy to blame God or someone else or ourselves. But we live in a fallen world, and bad things happen. When we have more loss than we think we can handle (and it's all more than we can handle. That's why we need God!), we feel somehow cheated by God. I hear of people who become atheists when God doesn't meet their expectations. The fact that we expect good seems to me to mean we know there is a God who is good.

I recently read an interesting quote by Timothy Keller. In a devotion on Psalm 89:9–18, he wrote, "Here are two attributes of God. He is all-powerful and He is perfectly righteous. To those confident of their own insight, suffering disproves the existence of such a God … But we should admit that an infinite God could have good reasons for allowing suffering that our finite minds can't fathom. Once we take the more humble stance, God's attributes are of deep comfort … The more I access (God's) goodness and control of things, the more I can relax."[2]

---

[2] Timothy and Kathy Keller, *The Songs of Jesus* (New York: Viking, 2015), 217.

Epilogue

Shawn and Karen live only a few miles away now. Isabel is eighteen. Timothy is thirty-three (and lives too far away!). He has a wonderful wife, Lauren, and they have a sweet new baby, Caroline.

The year after Matthew died, I was attending a choir workshop. A man shared a story of losing his wife and daughter several years earlier. I remember what he said. He spoke of the song, "The Longer I Serve Him, the Sweeter he grows." He said he could honestly sing those words and knew the truth of them. I heard the song recently and realized that what he said was true.

About five years after losing Paul, I ran into Howard, an old friend from college. Both of us were single then, and we started dating. It was such a joyful surprise to have such love at my age. We've now been married for five years. I am grateful that this godly man was given to me. We have connected more and more with old college friends these days, and it's such a blessing.

When we were in college, Howard and I sang in a group called The New Creations. One song we sang was Andre Crouch's "Through it All." A few years ago, at a women's convention, four of us who sang in the group were asked to sing that song. We did, and at some point in the song, all four of us realized what we had been through. Two of us had lost children. The other two had had cancer. But when we sang, "Through it all, through it all, I've learned to trust in Jesus," we also knew the truth of that, and it came over all of us at the same time. We'd all believed it when we had sung it as young adults. But now we knew it because we'd experienced it.

I'm learning to appreciate every season of life. I think we really embraced that with Timothy's childhood after losing Matthew. But all the seasons are temporary. Some are hard, but they will pass. Some are wonderful, but they'll pass also.

Time really does help. The sorrow is a part of you, but you can still have a joyful life. I've learned that we all heal in our own time and in our own way. Mostly, I've learned that God is still good and that He really can turn our sorrow into joy.

I want anyone who reads this to know that, for me, this is not so much a story of loss. It's a story of the presence of God in a life. It's a story of His faithfulness to us. It's a story of the God who sees and hears us and knows what we need and, even in sadness, provides joy. We have all struggled with sickness and loss (or we will). But I do know there is a God who is faithful and hears our cries to Him and can give us beauty for ashes and joy for mourning (Isaiah 61:3) if we just give him our mourning.

Think before you speak to people who are suffering or grieving. I almost wanted to write much more on inappropriate things people have said. Just being there is the best thing. Saying "I love you," or, "I'm praying for you," or even, "I don't know what to say," is okay.

On the other hand, if you are grieving, remember that people don't know what to say, and they feel like they have to say something. They're trying to be comforting and don't know how. My husband likes to say, "Remember their heart." People do have good intentions.

Honestly, there are so many examples of the kindness of people who helped us over and over during and after Paul's illness. I could see the hand of God in their kindness. Years before I met Paul, I got to know an elderly couple. She sent me birthday cards, Christmas cards, and sometimes just notes to say hello. So, we communicated by mail for years, and she learned about Paul and about Matthew. On my first wedding anniversary without Paul (two days after what would have been Matthew's birthday), she sent me a card with a note saying she was praying for me during these difficult days. I don't know if she remembered that there were two days I was grieving over at that time. Probably she did, but even if she didn't, she reminded me that God knew and cared. Never underestimate the value of a simple act of kindness.

We can be honest with God. It's OK to tell Him how we feel, even if we're mad with Him. He's bigger than all that.

Grief goes away and then suddenly returns, overwhelming us, sometimes seeming as painful as when it first happens. When I was writing my journal about Matthew, I was writing about losing him and the grief. I had to stop for a while, as I felt overwhelmed. I went to the cemetery and cried a while and went back home. Even now, as I was reviewing all of the story, I would sometimes need to leave it a while because it was too sad. But I know this. Joyful times will return as well. During dark moments, remind yourself of that.

Years ago, I read about a woman who had such great victory as a Christian that, when she lost her family members, she did not cry but rejoiced. I thought at the time, *How wonderful to be that way.* But in scripture, we see people setting aside time to grieve. And the apostle Paul said not to grieve as those who have no hope. We grieve, and we should allow ourselves to grieve, but we can still remind ourselves of the hope of seeing our loved ones—our treasures—in heaven again.

Printed in the United States
by Baker & Taylor Publisher Services